The Test Tutor:

Practice Test for the NNAT® 2

Level B
(First Grade)

Test Tutor Publishing, LLC

Practice Test for the NNAT®2 Test– Level B

Written and published by: Test Tutor Publishing, LLC

Printed in the United States of America
September 2012

TABLE OF CONTENTS

Naglieri Nonverbal Ability Test®2 Explained

The *Naglieri Nonverbal Ability Test® 2nd edition (NNAT®2)* is the new and revised edition of the *Naglieri Nonverbal Ability Test® — Multilevel Form.*

The NNAT®2 test is designed to measure general ability as a predictor of academic success in children ages 5 to 17 years old. The test uses nonverbal methods in the form of figure matrices. As a nonverbal test, it requires no verbal, reading or math skills, making it a fair assessment of ability regardless of culture, language, or motor and/or communication disability.

The test is comprised of seven levels spanning the ages of 5 to 17 and grades K through 12. The following table details the test levels based on grade.

NNAT®2 Test Grades and Levels

Grade	Level
K	**A**
1	**B**
2	**C**
3 and 4	**D**
5 and 6	**E**
7, 8, and 9	**F**
10, 11, and 12	**G**

NNAT®2 Test Administration

- Administered in a group setting with paper and pencil or on the computer
- No reading or speaking is required
- 30 minute time limit
- 48 questions in each level

Differences between NNAT® —Multilevel and NNAT®2 Test

- Redesigned to engage and better assess the general population.
- Available for online administration.
- NNAT®2 test contains 48 questions rather than 38 to be completed within the original 30-minute time limit.

How the NNAT®2 Test is scored

The raw score is calculated based on the number of questions the child answered correctly. The raw score is converted to a scaled score, which is then converted to a Naglieri Ability Index (NAI) by age in three-month intervals. The NAI scores are set at a mean of 100 based on the child's age. The lowest NAI score is 50; the highest is 150.

Percentile ranks range from 1 to 99 and describe a child's performance relative to other students in the same age group. For example, a child performing in the 99th percentile scored higher than 99% of the students in the same age group. The average rank falls between the 25th and 75th percentiles. This workbook is not designed to give a test score or rank because it has not been standardized with NNAT®2 norms and standards.

How To Use This Practice Test

The Test Tutor: Practice Test for the NNAT®2 Test was developed to help children perform to the best of their abilities on the NNAT®2 test. It is a workbook designed to give your child ample practice and familiarity with the problem solving strategies necessary for success on the NNAT®2 test. Please note: This practice test is not designed to give a test score or rank because it has not been standardized with NNAT®2 test norms and standards.

Before you begin test preparation, thoroughly read through the book. **Gather several sharpened pencils and a timer** before sitting down with your child at a table in a quiet, well-lit room. First, explain the four types of questions that your child will find on the test. Make sure he/she understands the sample questions before moving on to the practice test.

Tips for Testing Success

1. **Pay careful attention to the instructions given during the examination**. This will prevent unnecessary mistakes that will lower the test score.
2. **Look over all of the answer choices before selecting an answer**. NNAT®2 test is a multiple choice test. Do not rush when selecting an answer. Take the time to select the best answer.
3. **Eliminate obviously wrong answers**. Then select the best answer from among the remaining choices. Doing this will improve the odds of selecting the correct answer.
4. **Guess**. If, after eliminating the obviously wrong choices, you do not know the correct answer, just guess. NNAT®2 test scores are based on the number of correct answers. Students are not penalized for incorrect answers. Therefore, DO NOT LEAVE ANY QUESTIONS BLANK. If you skip questions, make sure you leave enough time to return to them.

NNAT®2 Test Question Types

The NNAT®2 test contains four types of questions:

1. Pattern Completion

As the easiest type of question to solve, pattern completion questions will be found primarily in the lower grade levels. The child will be presented with a rectangular design containing a missing piece. To solve the puzzle, the child must look at the design with a missing piece and select the answer that completes the pattern. For example:

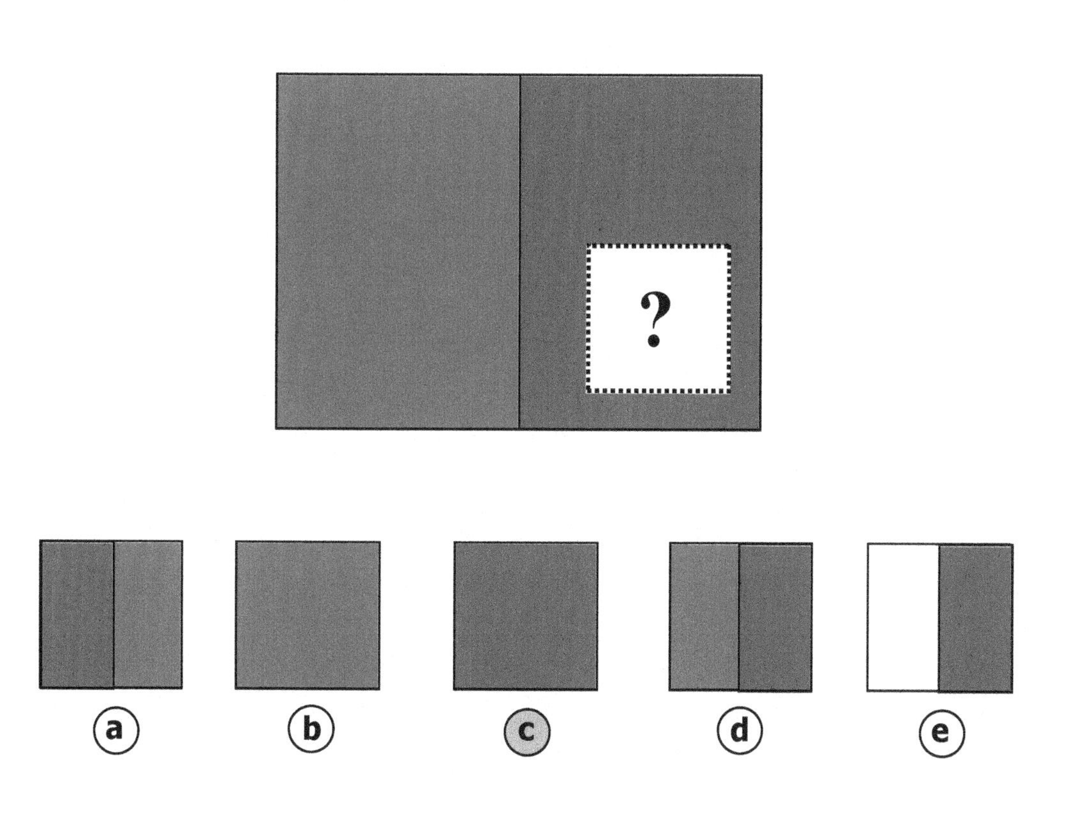

2. Reasoning by Analogy

In this exercise, the child will be presented with two or three rows of objects that comprise a matrix. The child must recognize how objects within the columns and rows change as one moves across or down the matrix. For example:

 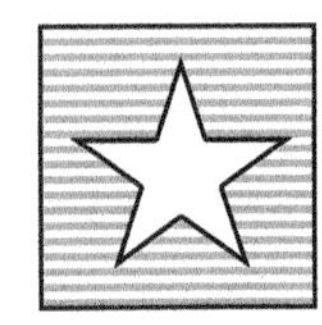

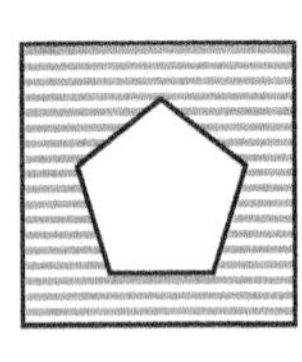 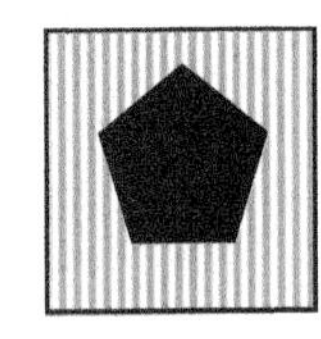  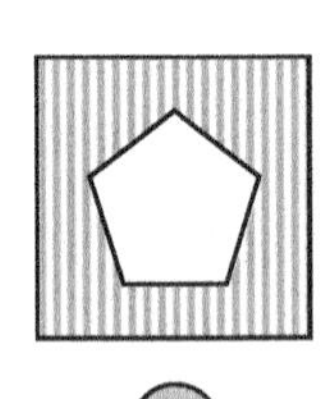 

a b c d e

3. Serial Reasoning

In this type of exercise, the child must recognize how the shapes in the matrix change across the rows and down the columns. As the shapes change from row to row and column to column, each shape appears only once in each row and column. For example:

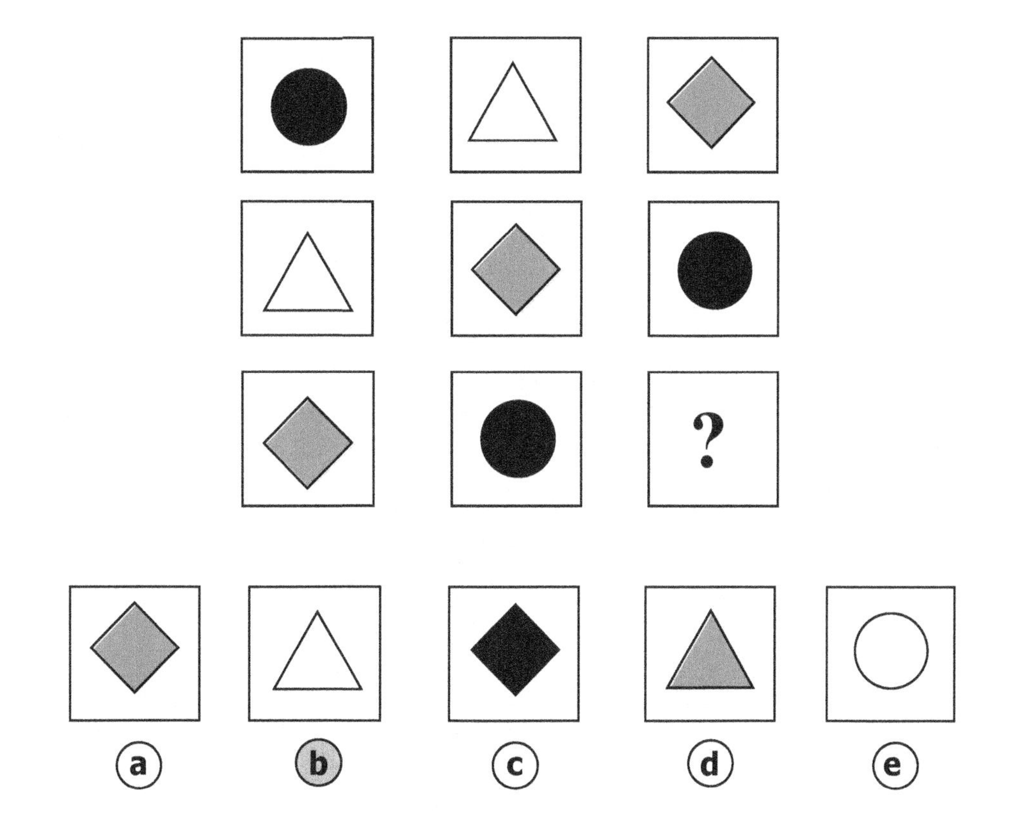

4. Spatial Visualization

Because spatial visualization exercises are the most difficult exercises in the NNAT®2, they will be found primarily in the upper grade level tests. To solve these exercises, the child must determine what two or more designs would look like if they were combined. For example:

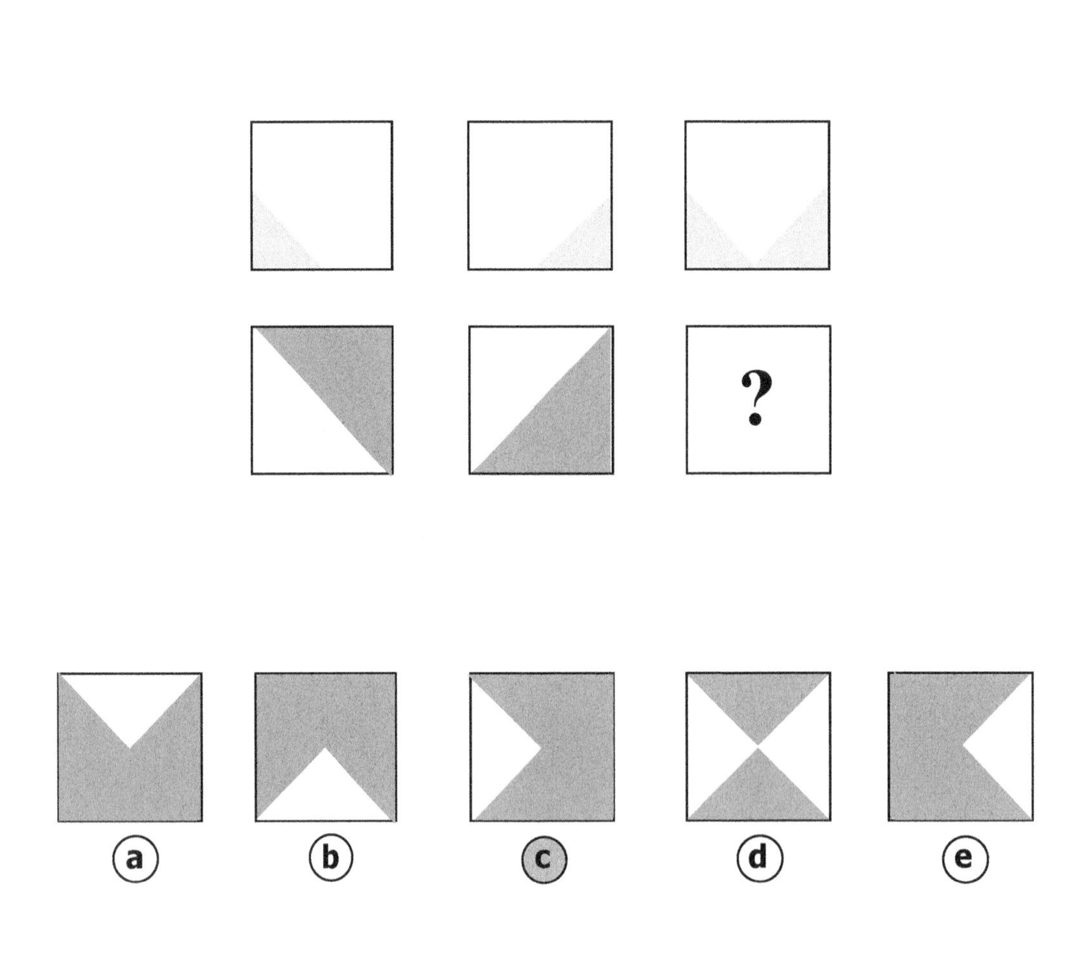

Practice Test Instructions

Sample #1

SAY: **Look at the big rectangle below. A part of it is missing. Find the piece that is missing among the answer choices below.**

Pause to allow the child to point to an answer.

SAY: **Very good. The missing piece is the square with an orange rectangle in the middle and two green rectangles on either side, which is letter c. Fill in the circle with the letter c.**

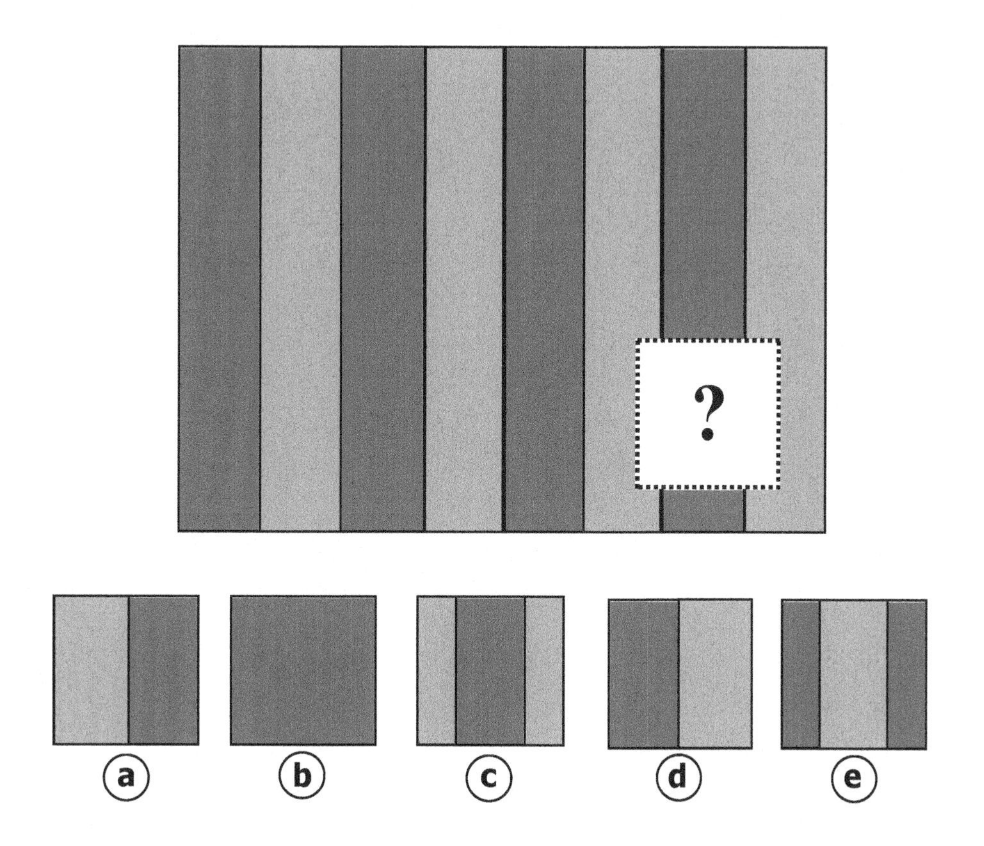

Sample #2

SAY: **Look at the four squares below. One square contains a question mark. Find the square that should go in the question mark box among the answer choices below.**

Pause to allow the child to point to an answer.

SAY: **The correct answer is the red arrow pointing up, which is letter a. Look at how the squares change across the rows. In the top row, the diamond shape changed its color from white to red. So, in the second row, the arrow should also change its color from white to red. Therefore, the correct answer is letter a. Fill in the circle with the letter a.**

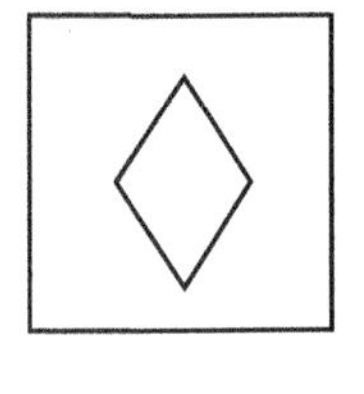
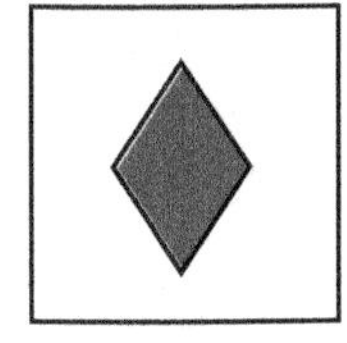
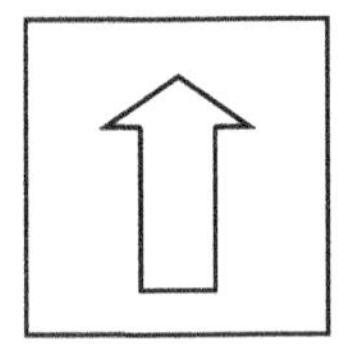

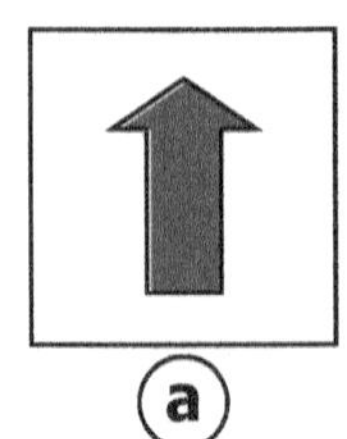
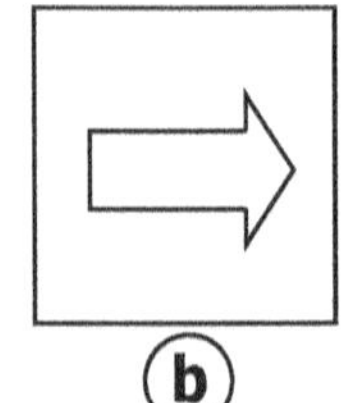
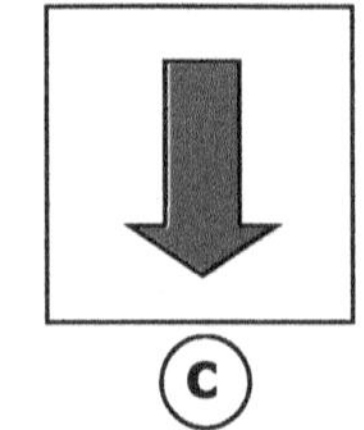
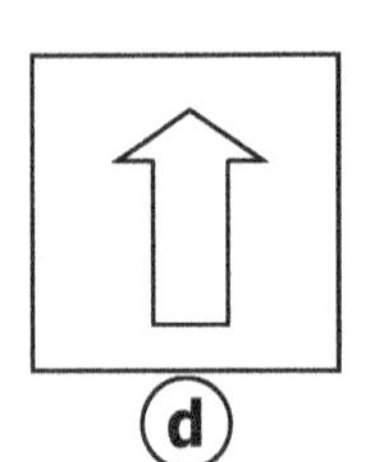
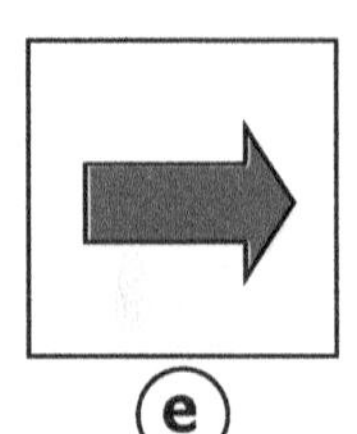

(a) (b) (c) (d) (e)

Sample #3

SAY: **Look at the squares below. One square contains a question mark. Find the square that should go in the question mark box among the answer choices below.**

Pause to allow the child to point to an answer.

SAY: **The correct answer is the blue triangle inside the white box, which is letter b. Fill in the circle with the letter b.**

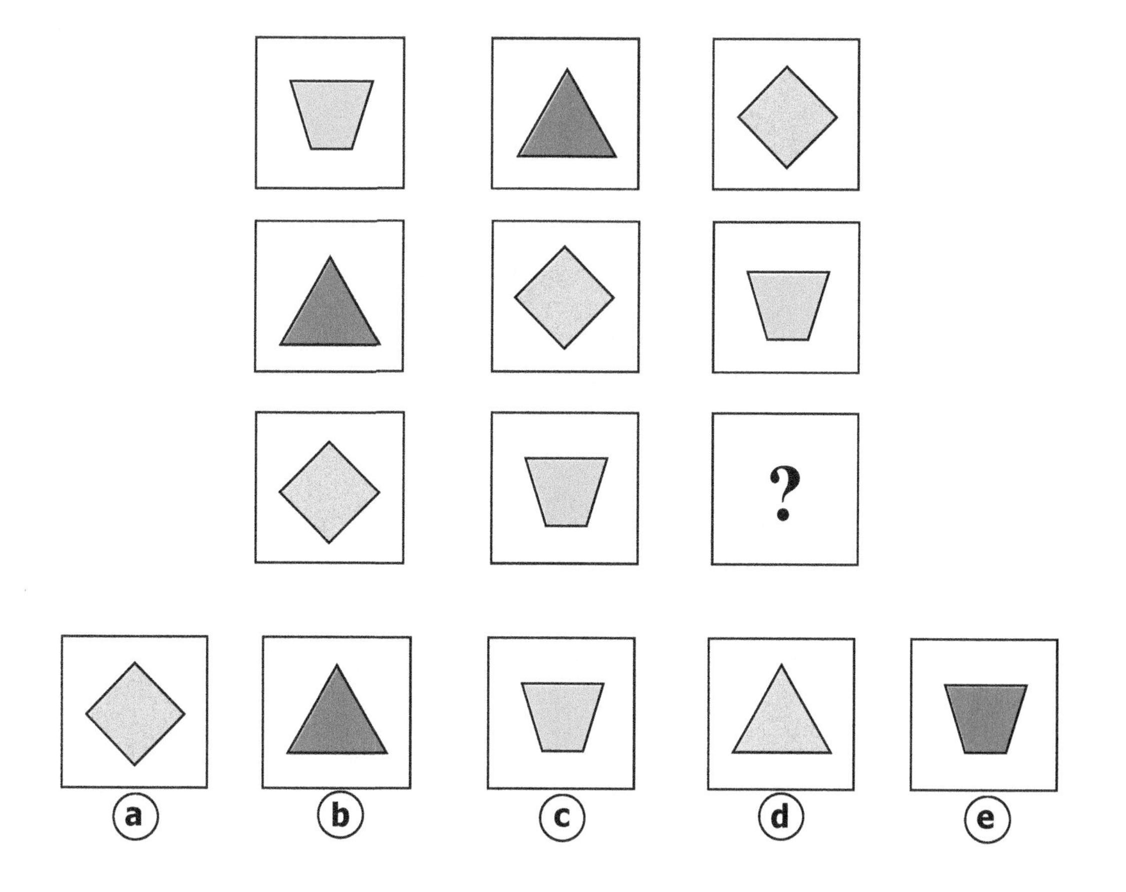

Sample #4

SAY: **Look at the squares below. One square contains a question mark. Find the square that should go in the question mark box among the answer choices below.**

Pause to allow the child to point to an answer.

SAY: **The correct answer is letter c. To solve this type of question you must imagine how the squares would look if they were combined. In this case, the blue squares are combined and then rotated clockwise. If the red triangles are combined and rotated the same way, the correct answer is letter c. Fill in the circle with the letter c.**

Now, go to the next page and complete all of the questions like these sample questions.

Begin timing and allow 30 minutes for your child to complete the test. When finished, check your child's answers with the answer key on page 48.

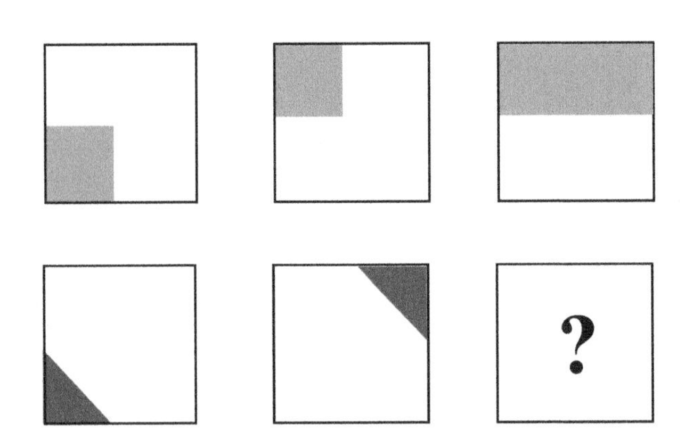

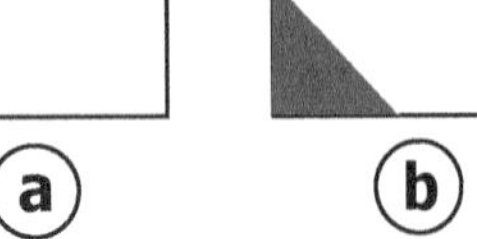
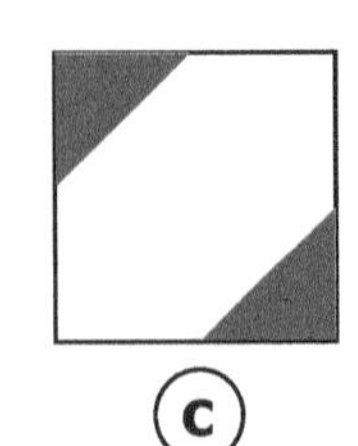
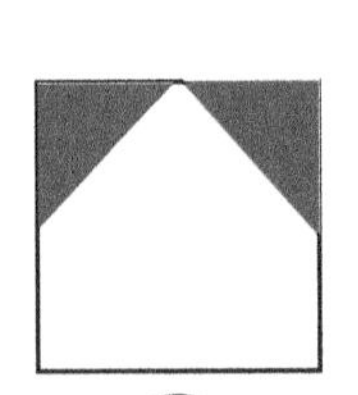
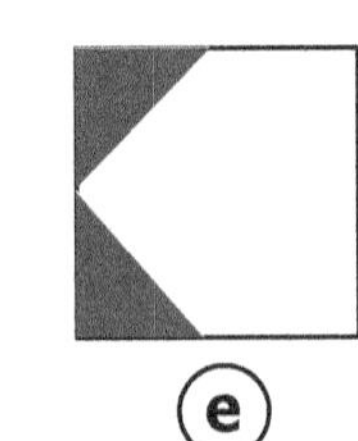

a b c d e

1.

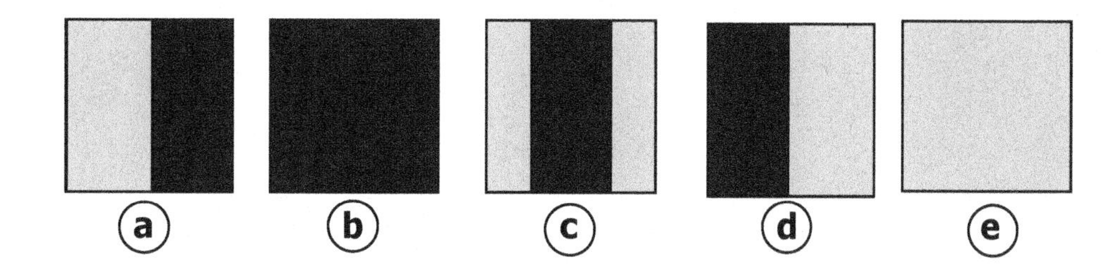

2.

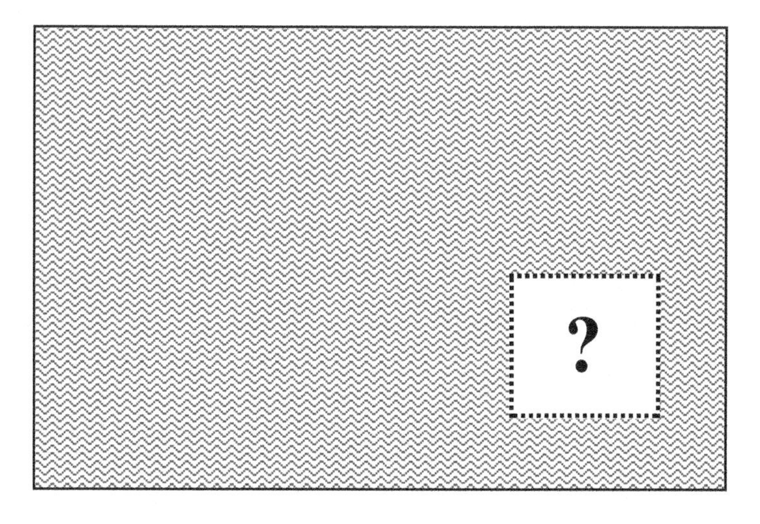

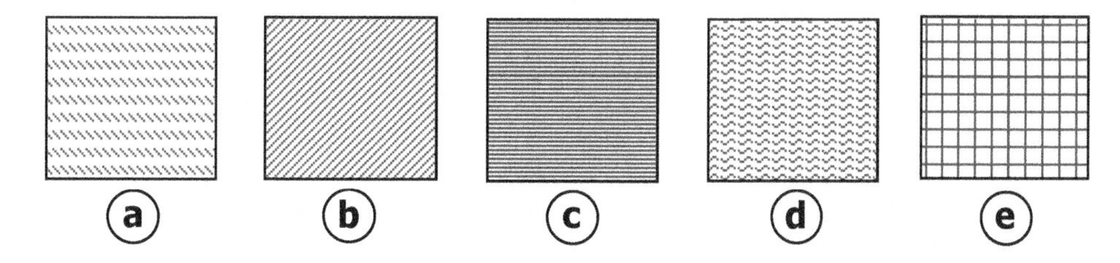

3.

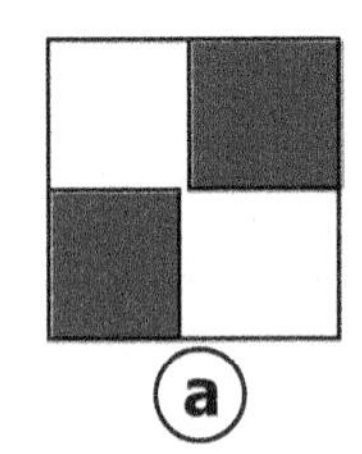
a

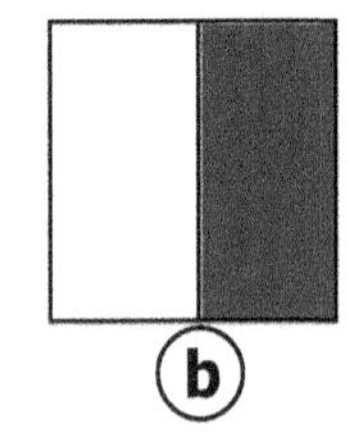
b

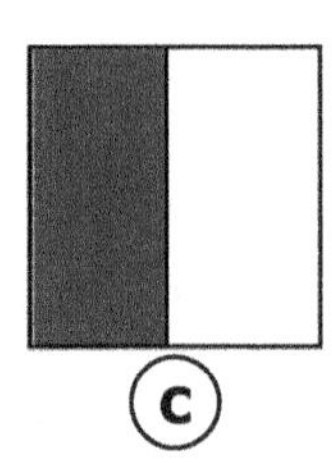
c

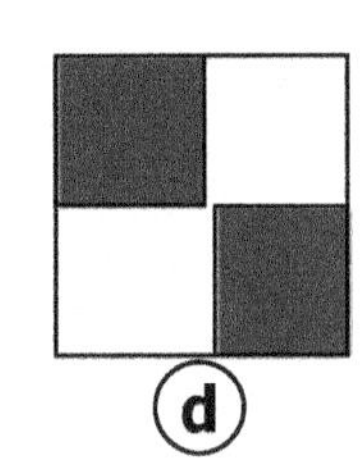
d

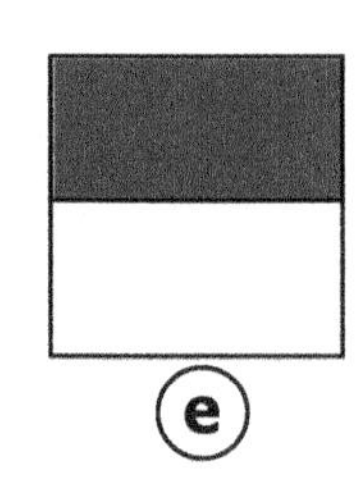
e

4.

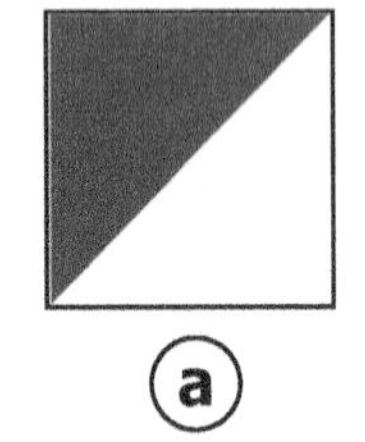
a

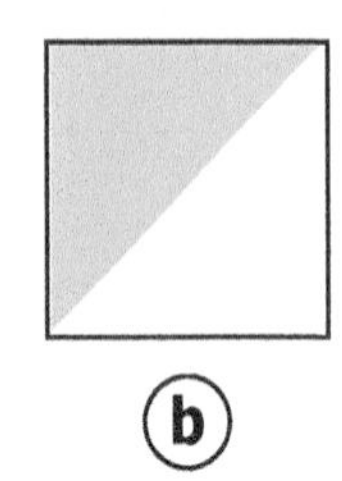
b

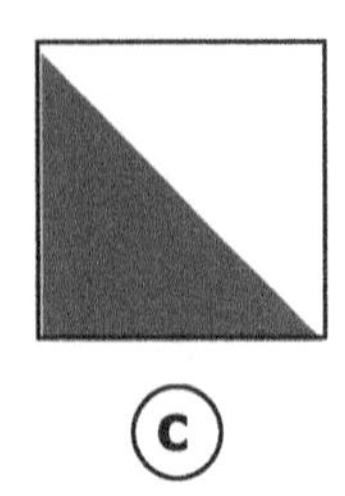
c

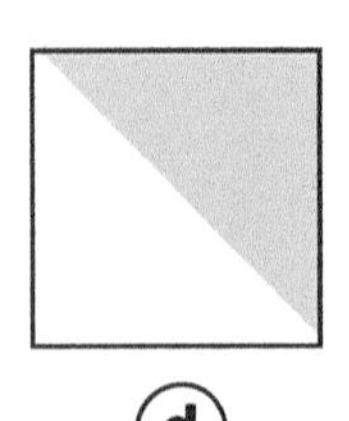
d

e

5.

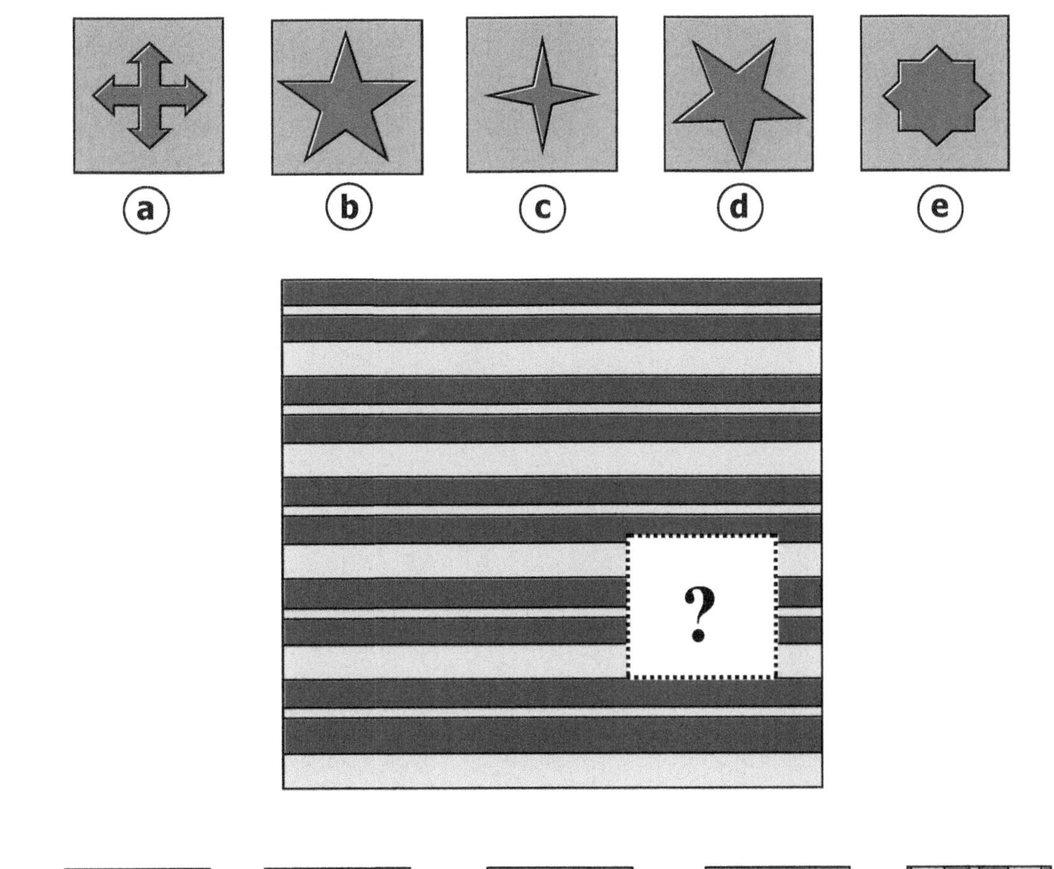

a b c d e

7.

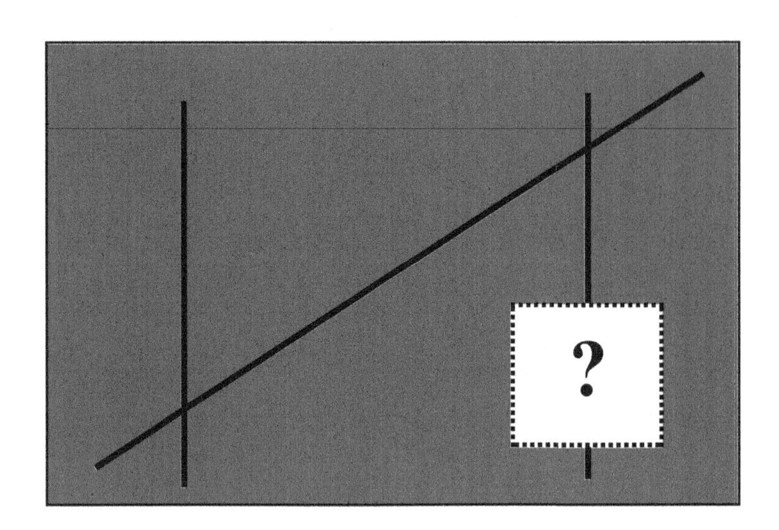

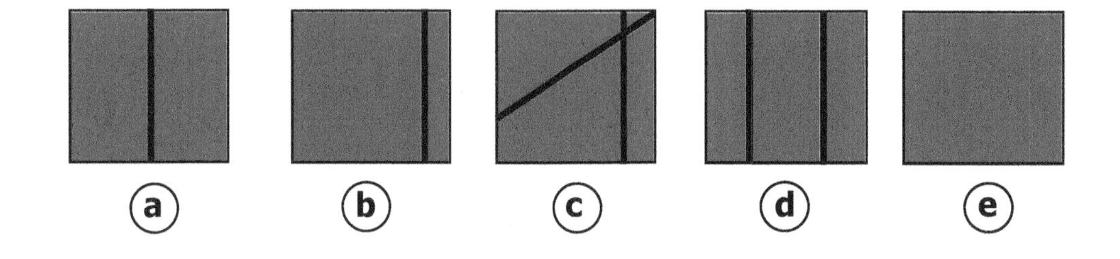

8.

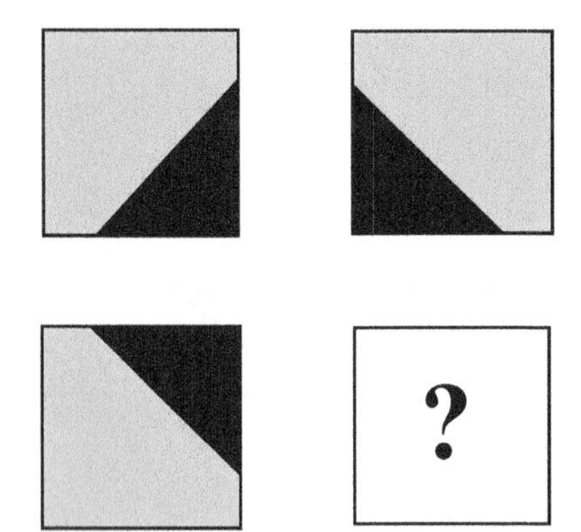

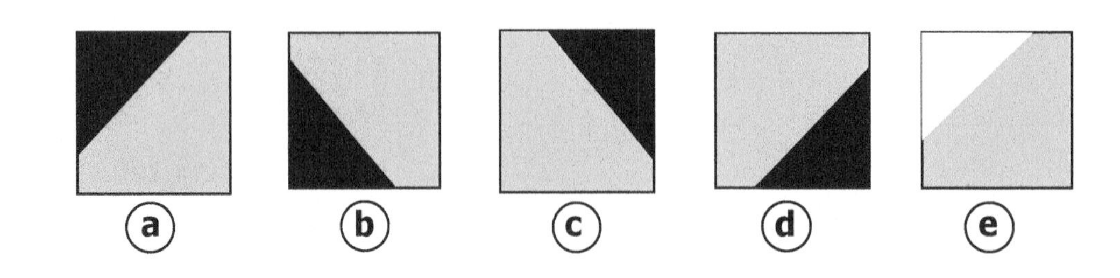

9.

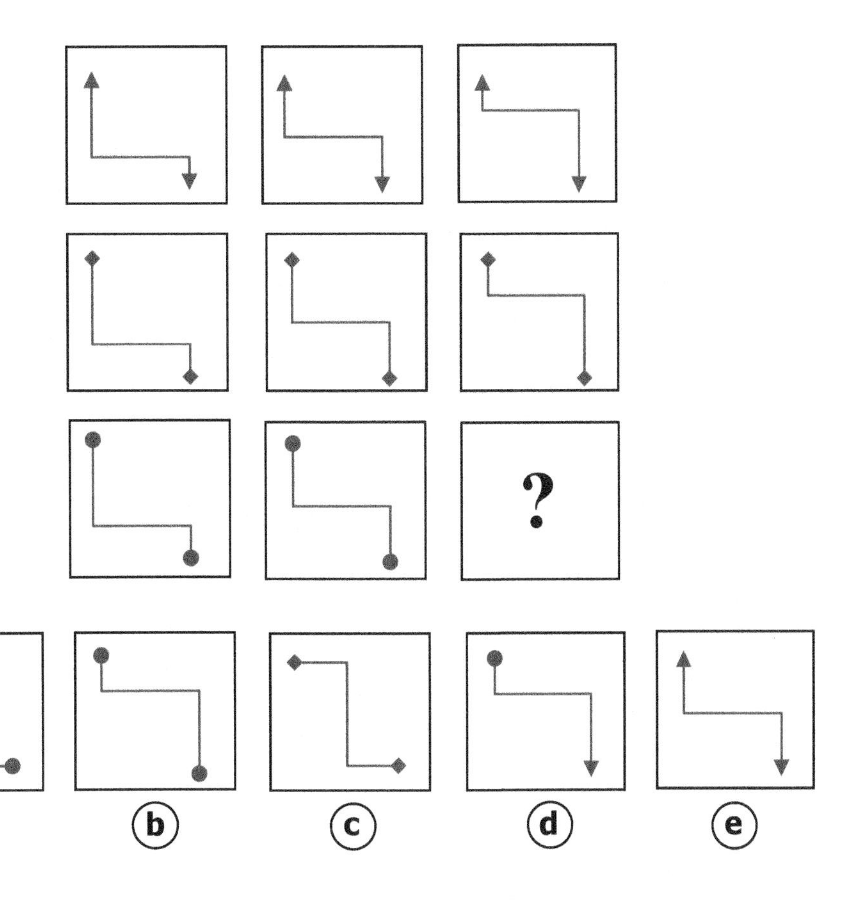

10.

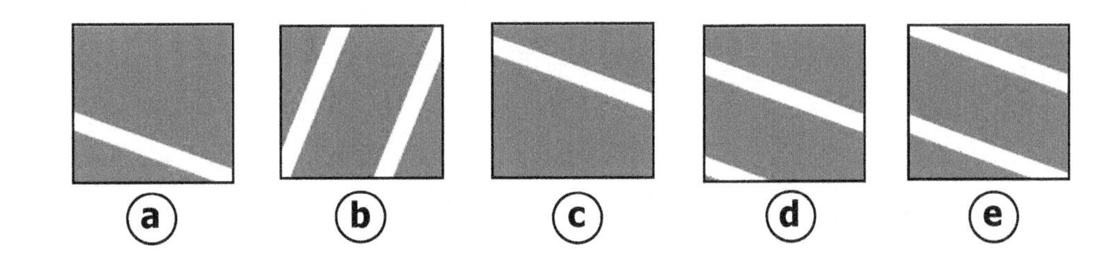

11.

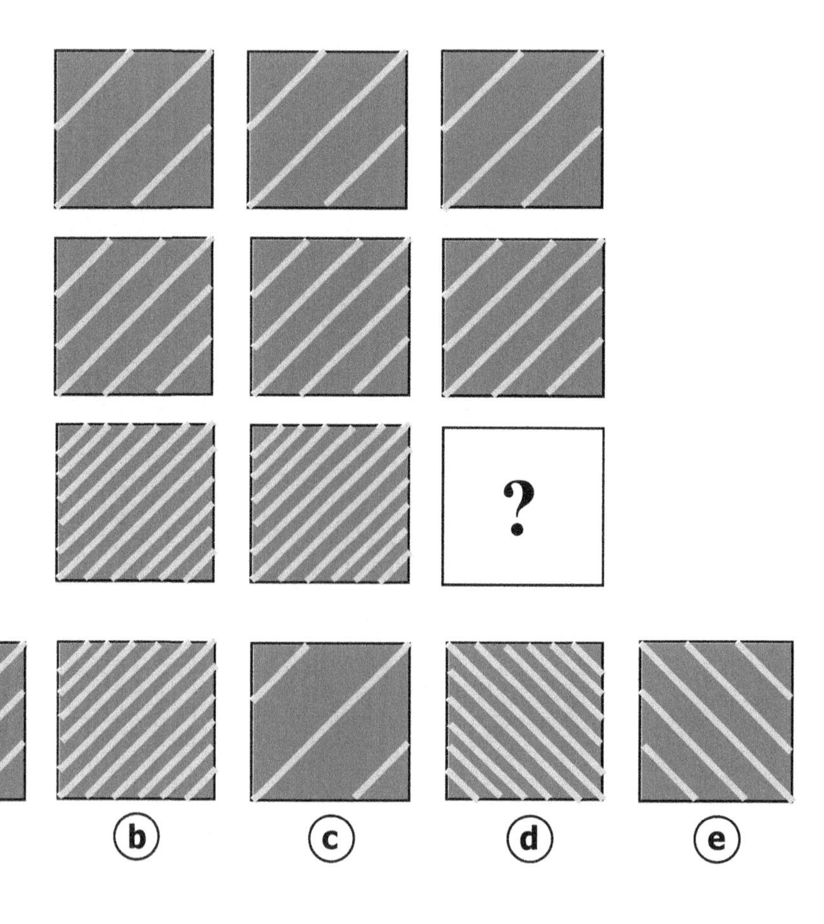

12.

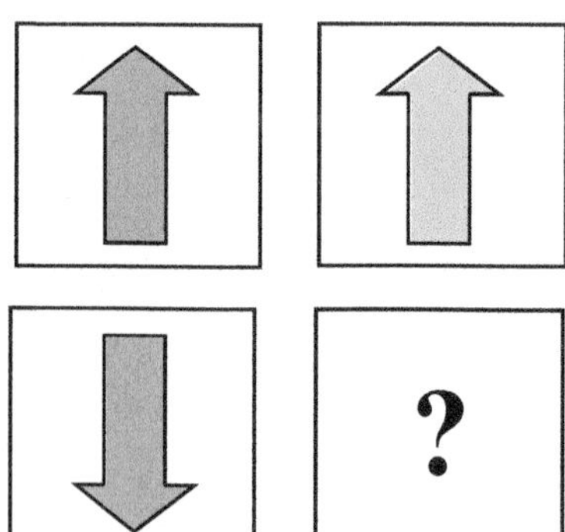

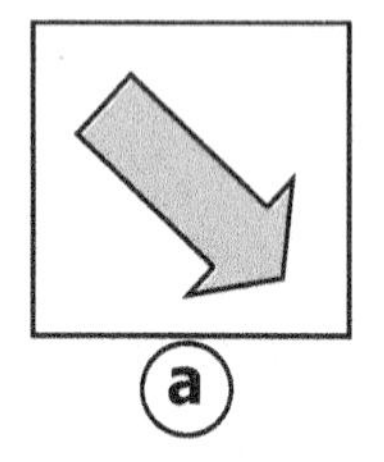

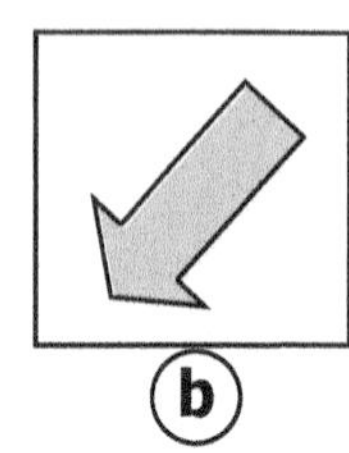

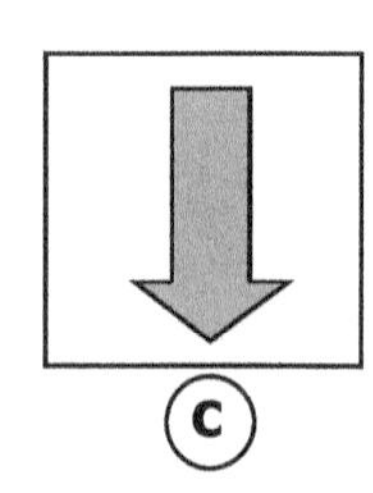

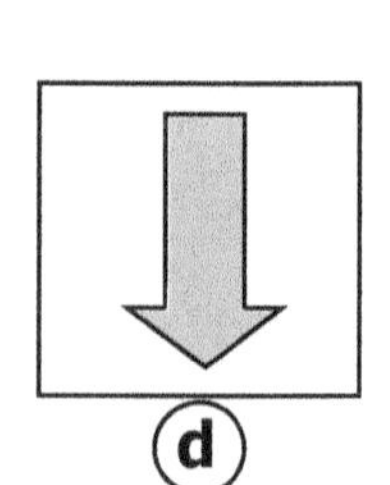

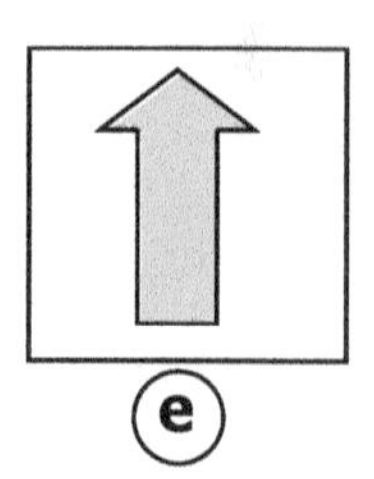

a b c d e

13.

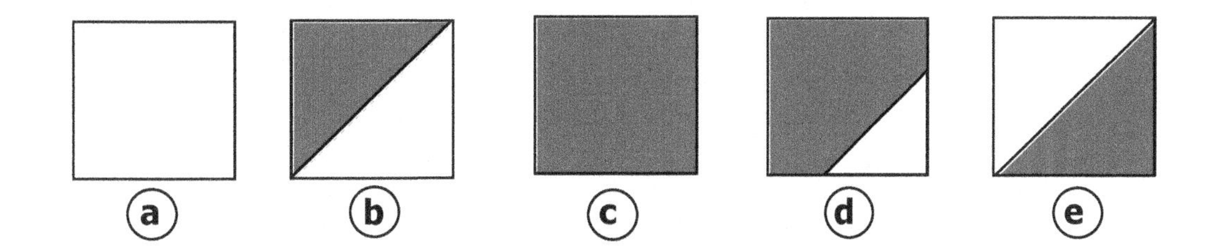

14.

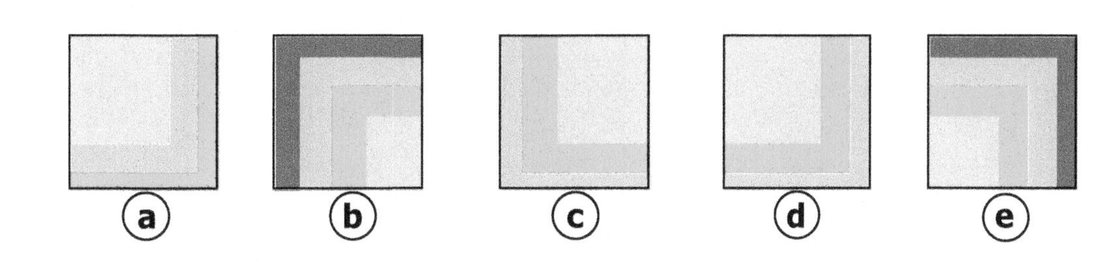

15.

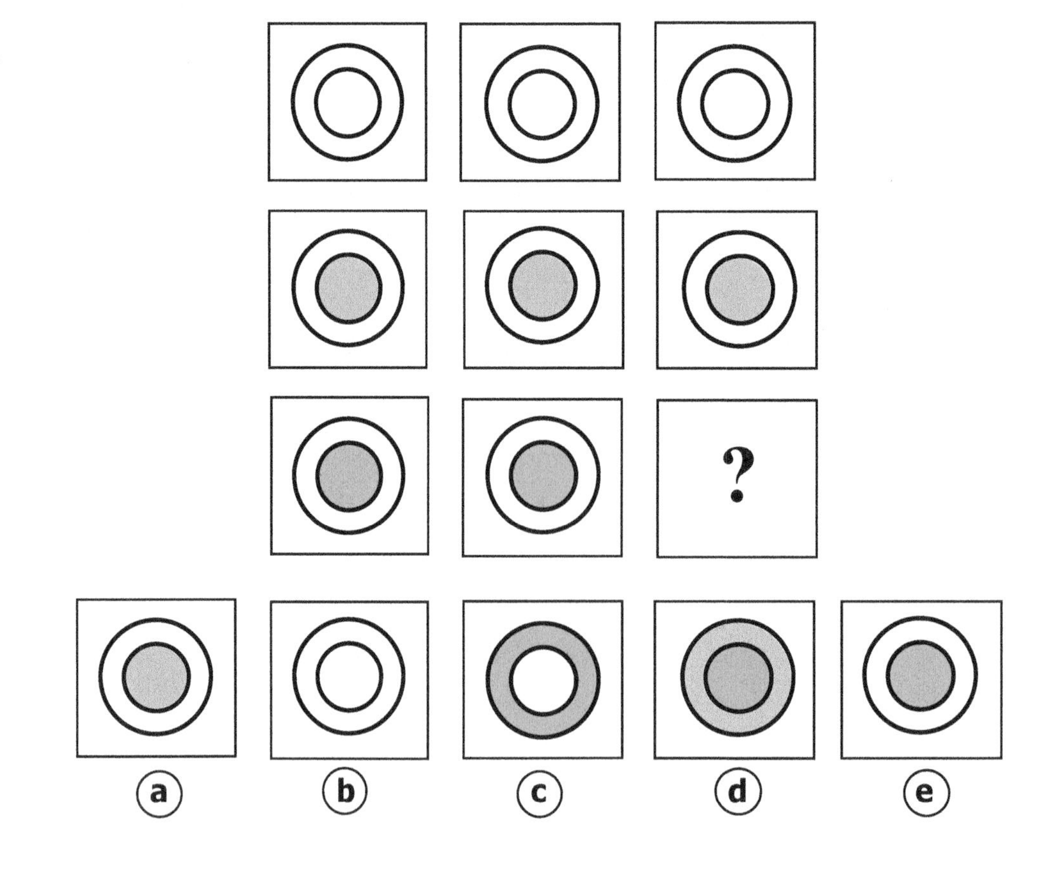

16.

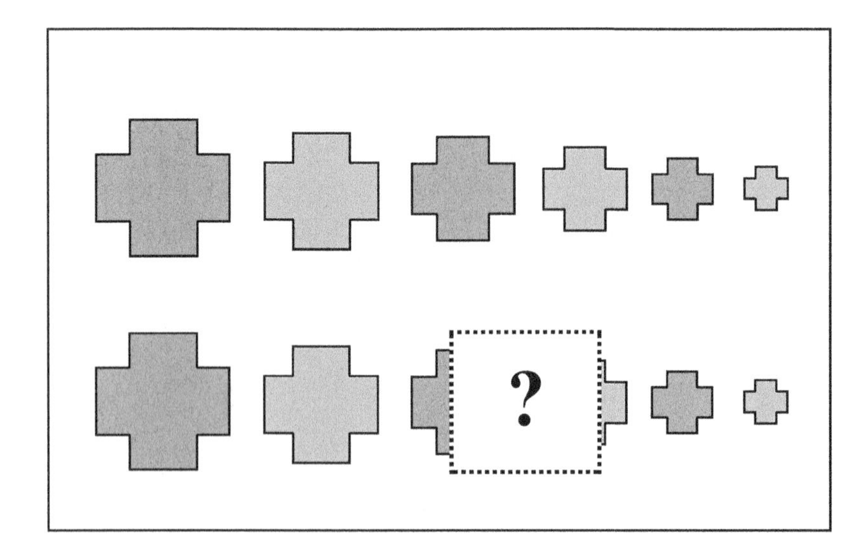

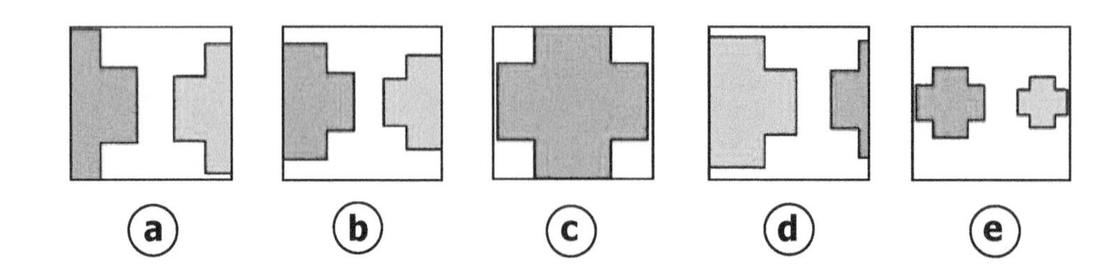

17.

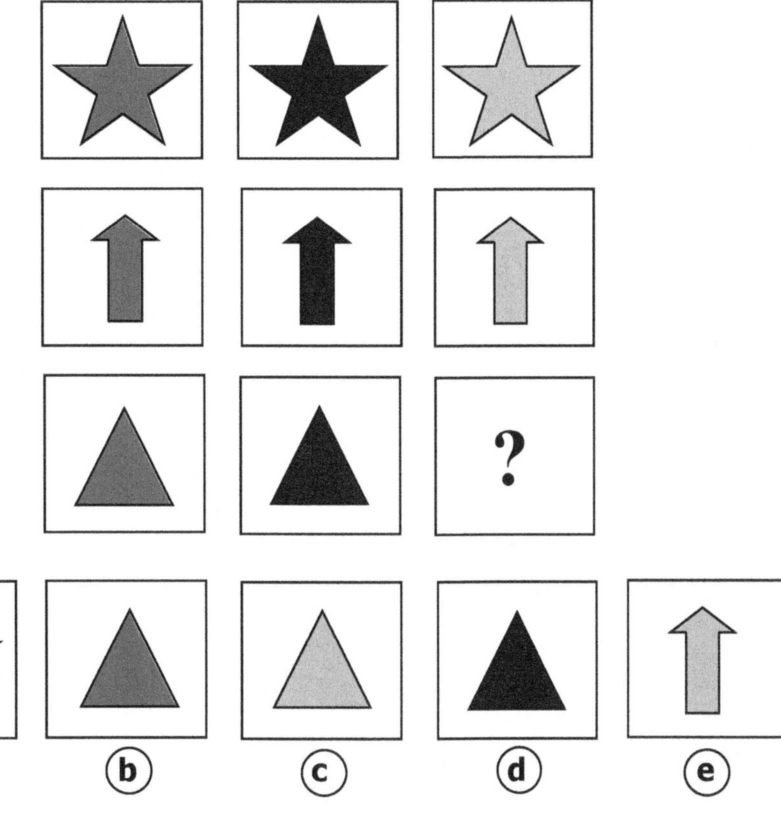

18.

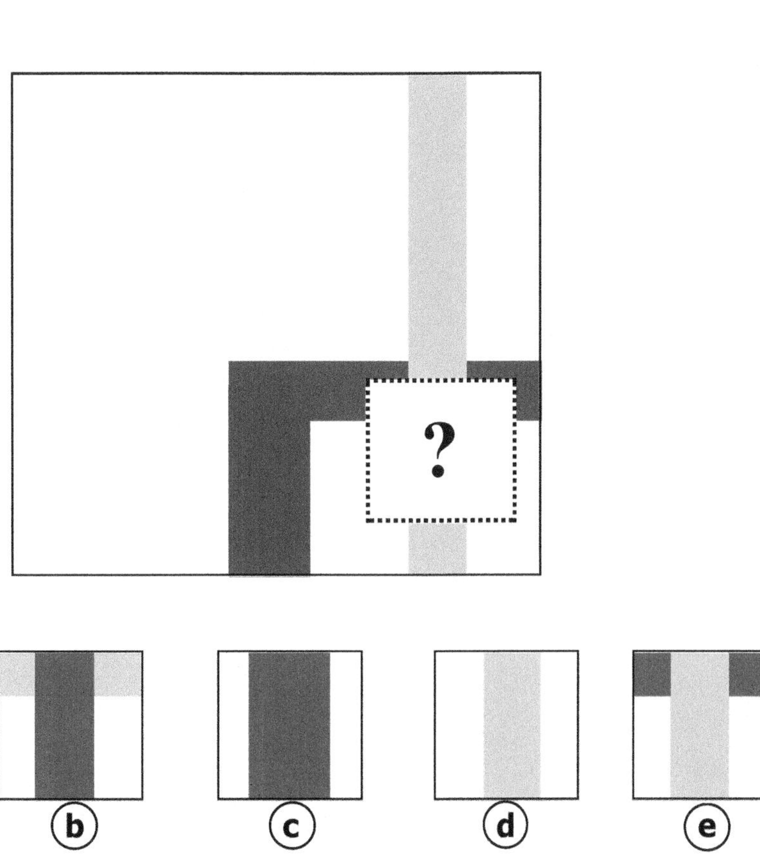

19.

(a)

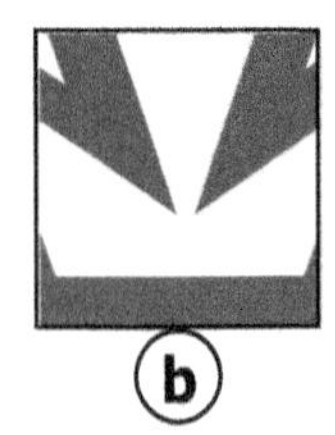
(b)

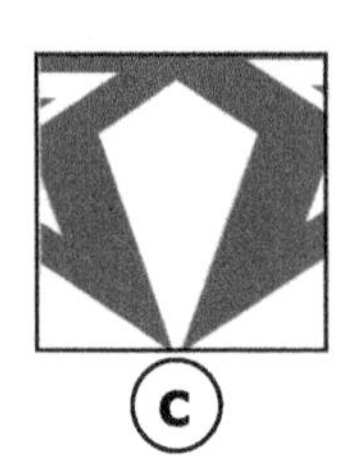
(c)

(d)

(e)

20.

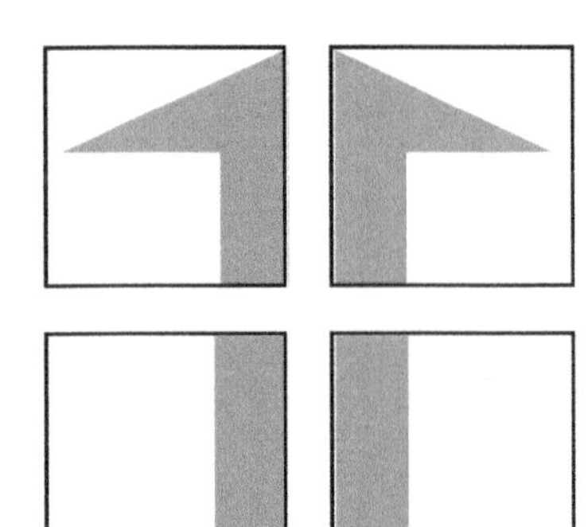

?

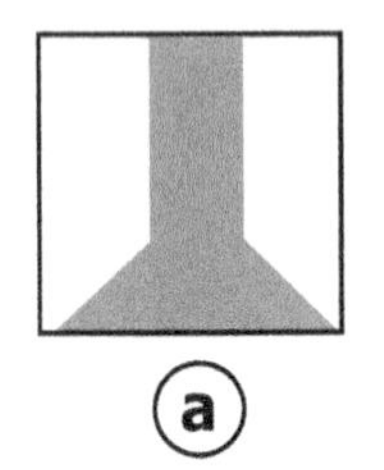
(a)

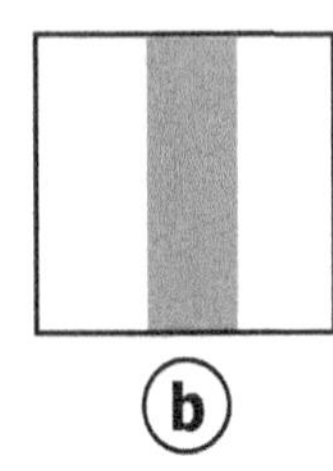
(b)

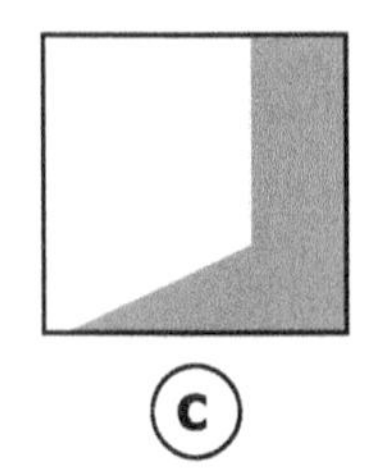
(c)

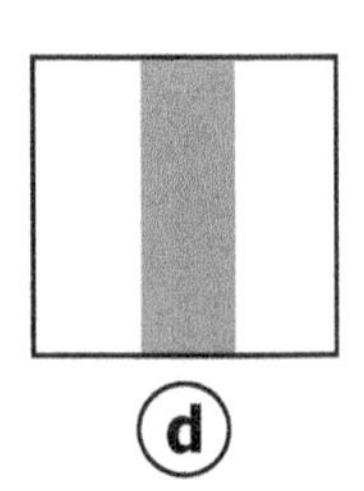
(d)

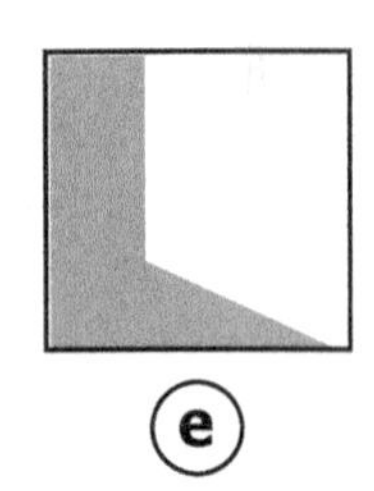
(e)

21.

(a)

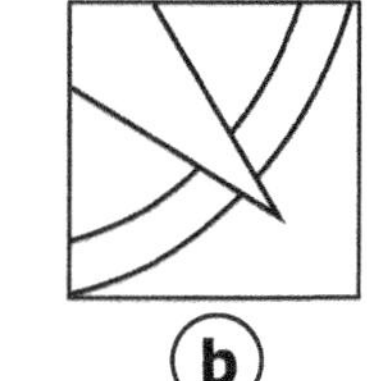

(b)

(c)

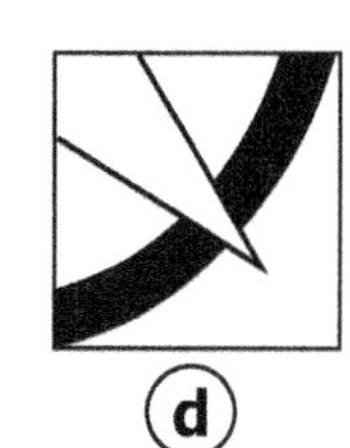

(d)

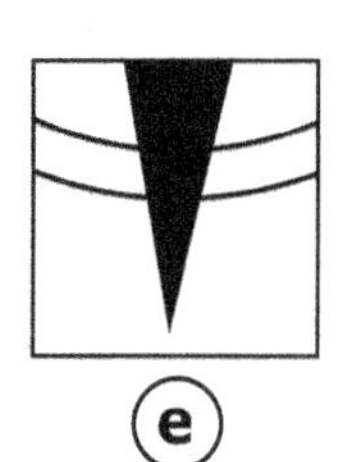

(e)

22.

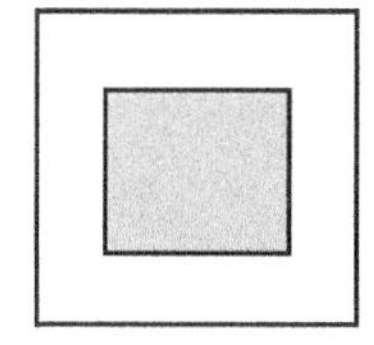

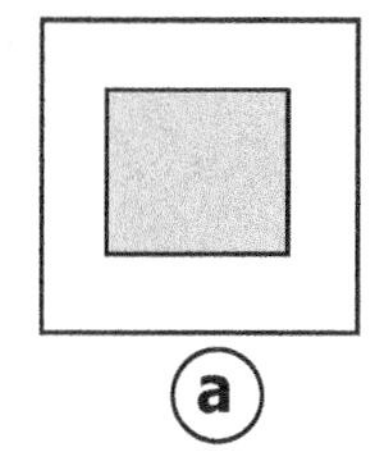

(a)

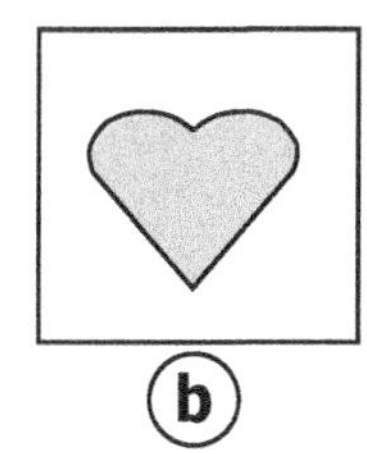

(b)

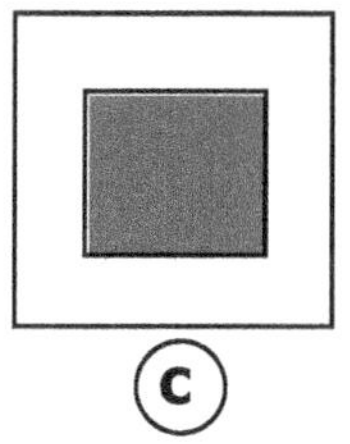

(c)

(d)

(e)

23.

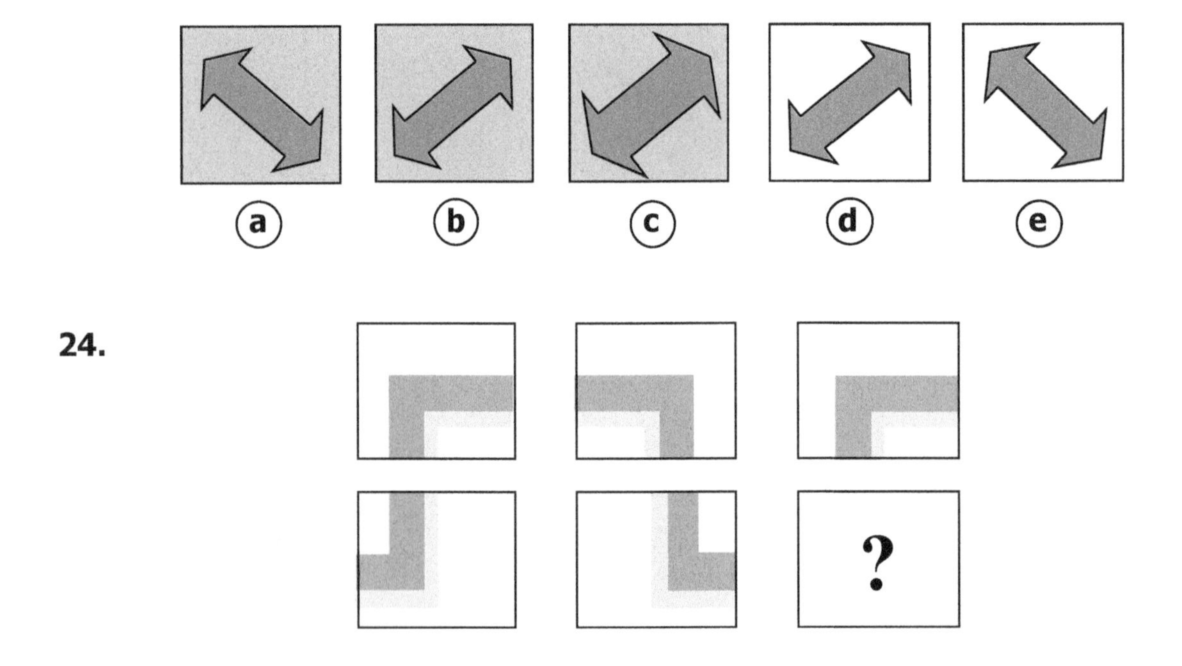

24.

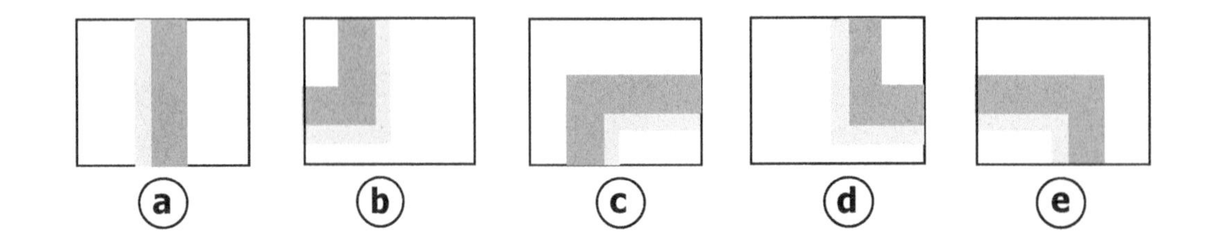

25.

?

(a) (b) (c) (d) (e)

26.

?

(a) (b) (c) (d) (e)

27.

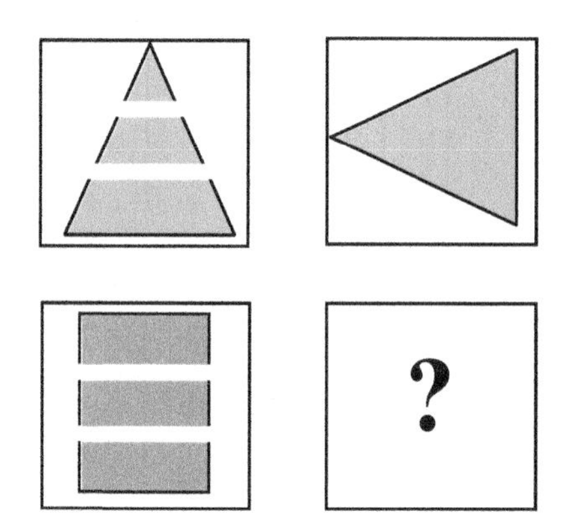

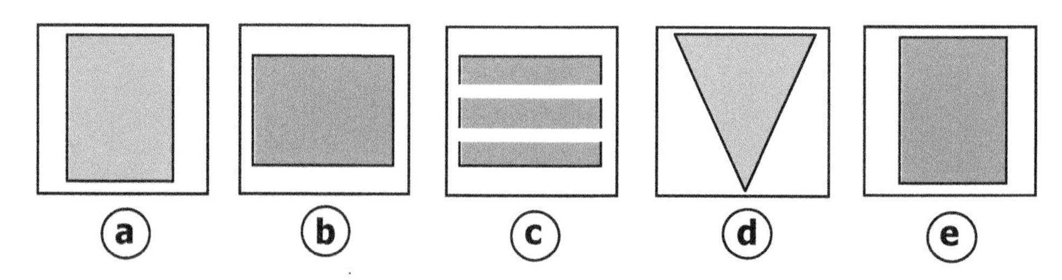

28.

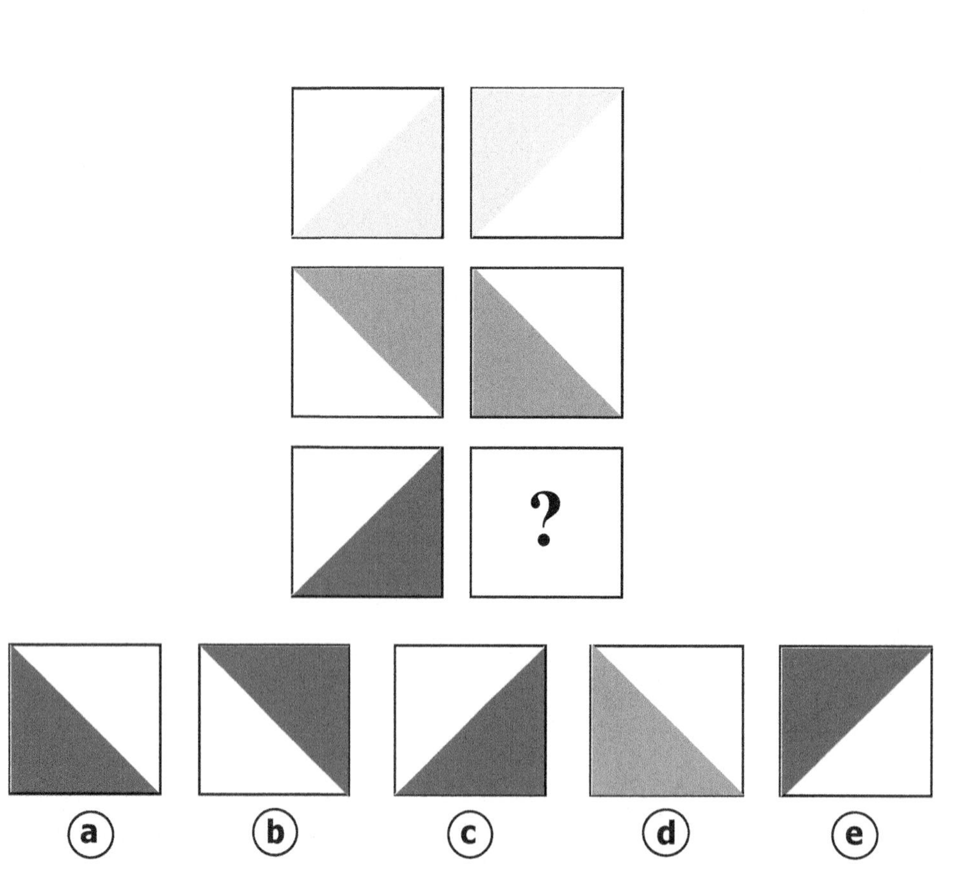

29.

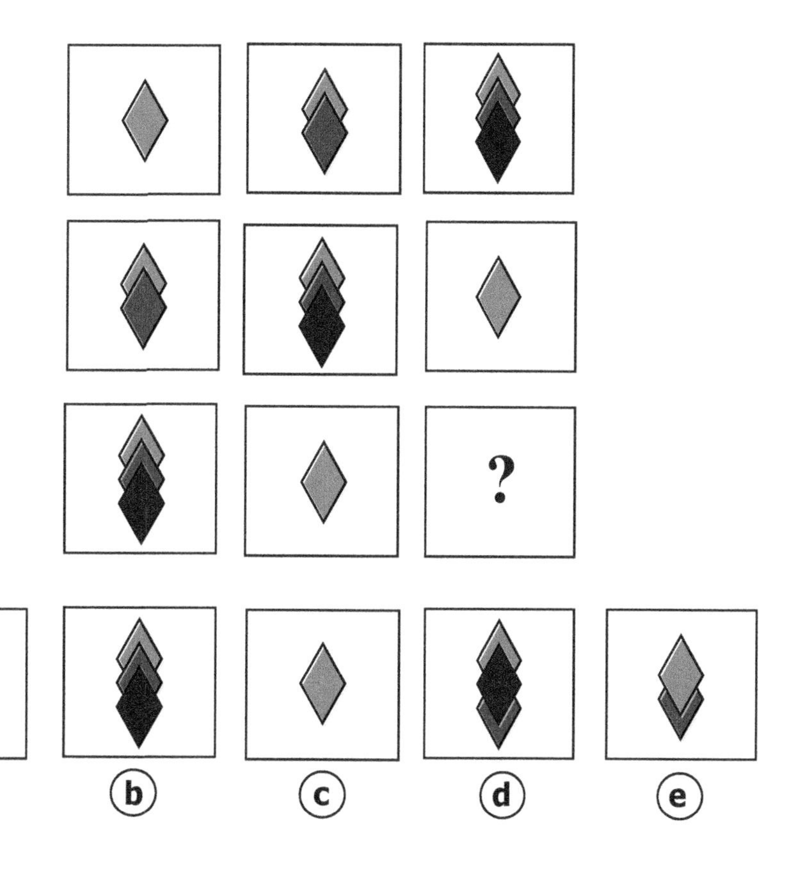

30.

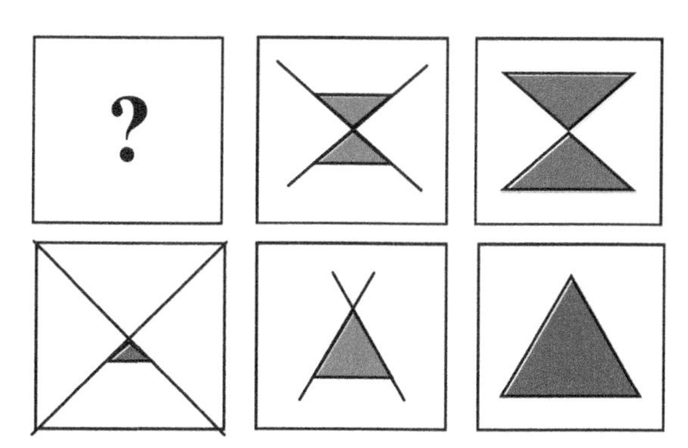

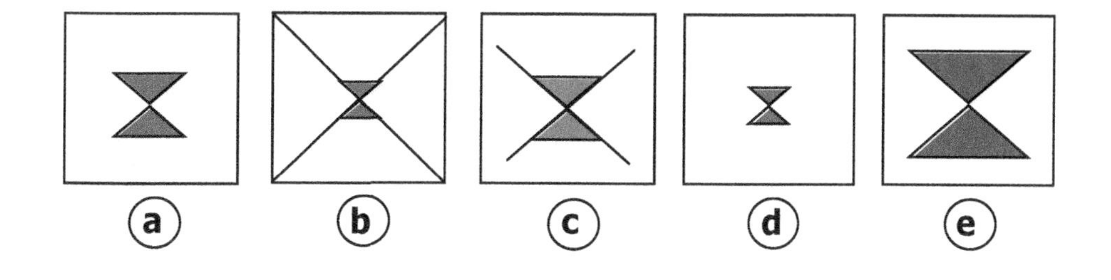

31.

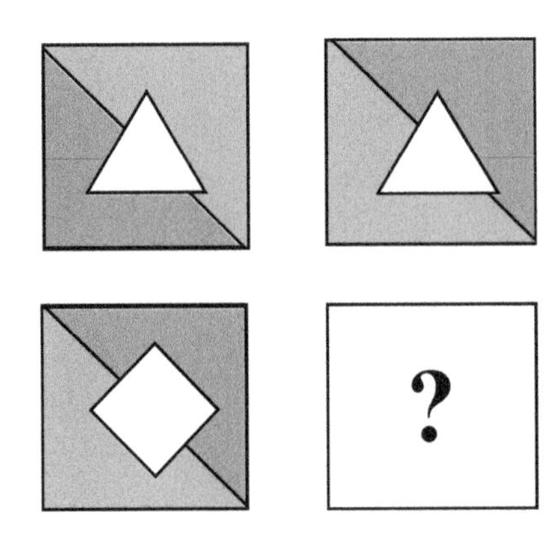

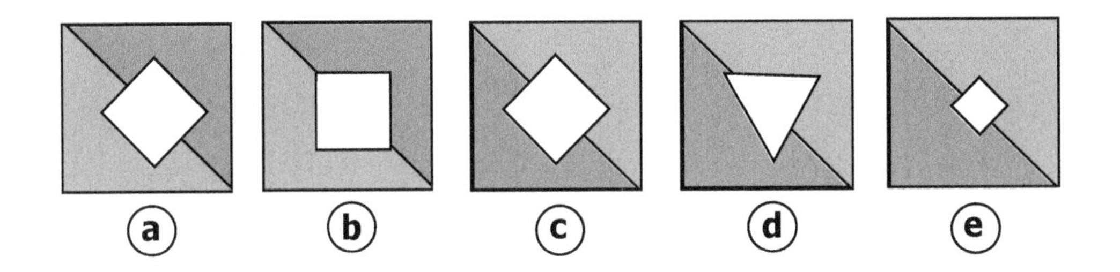

32.

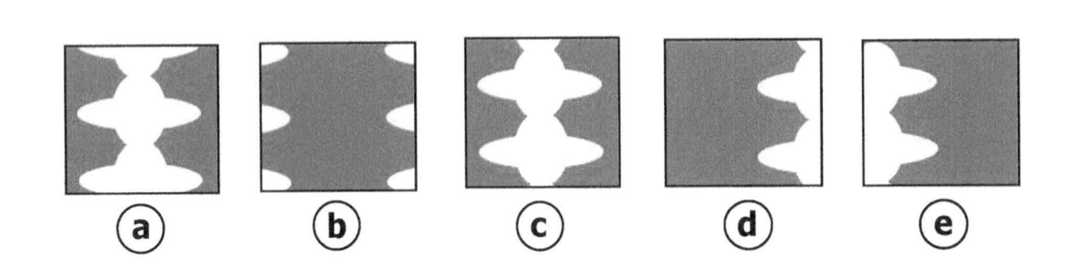

33.

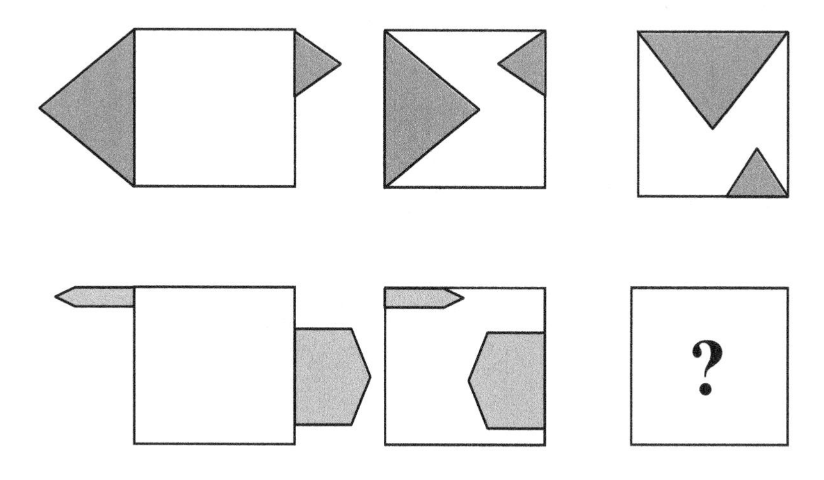

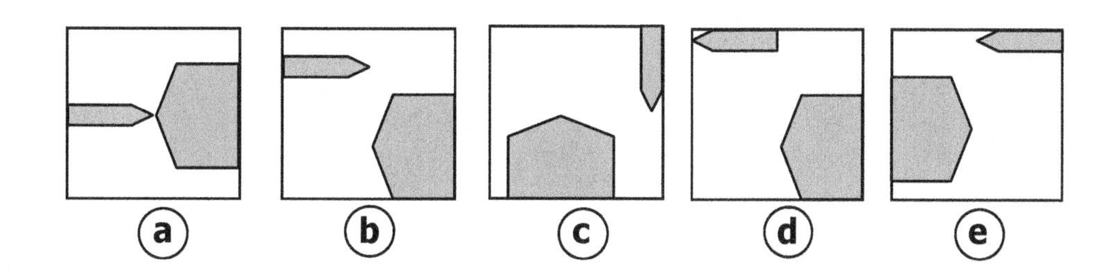

34.

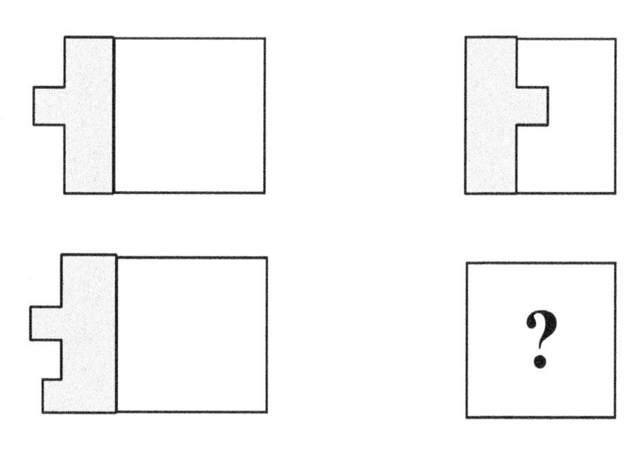

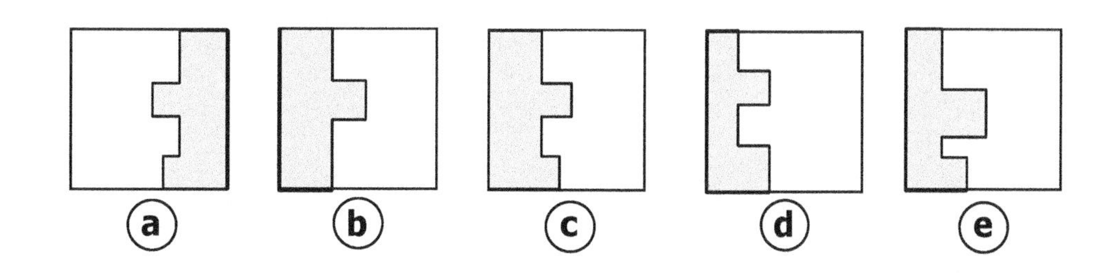

35.

?

a b c d e

36.

?

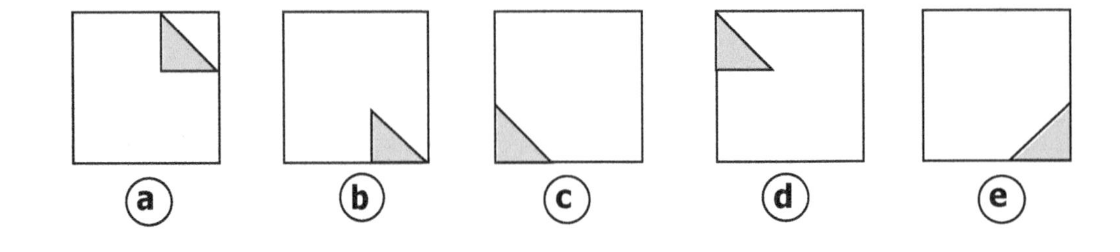

37.

?

(a) (b) (c) (d) (e)

38.

?

(a) (b) (c) (d) (e)

39.

40.

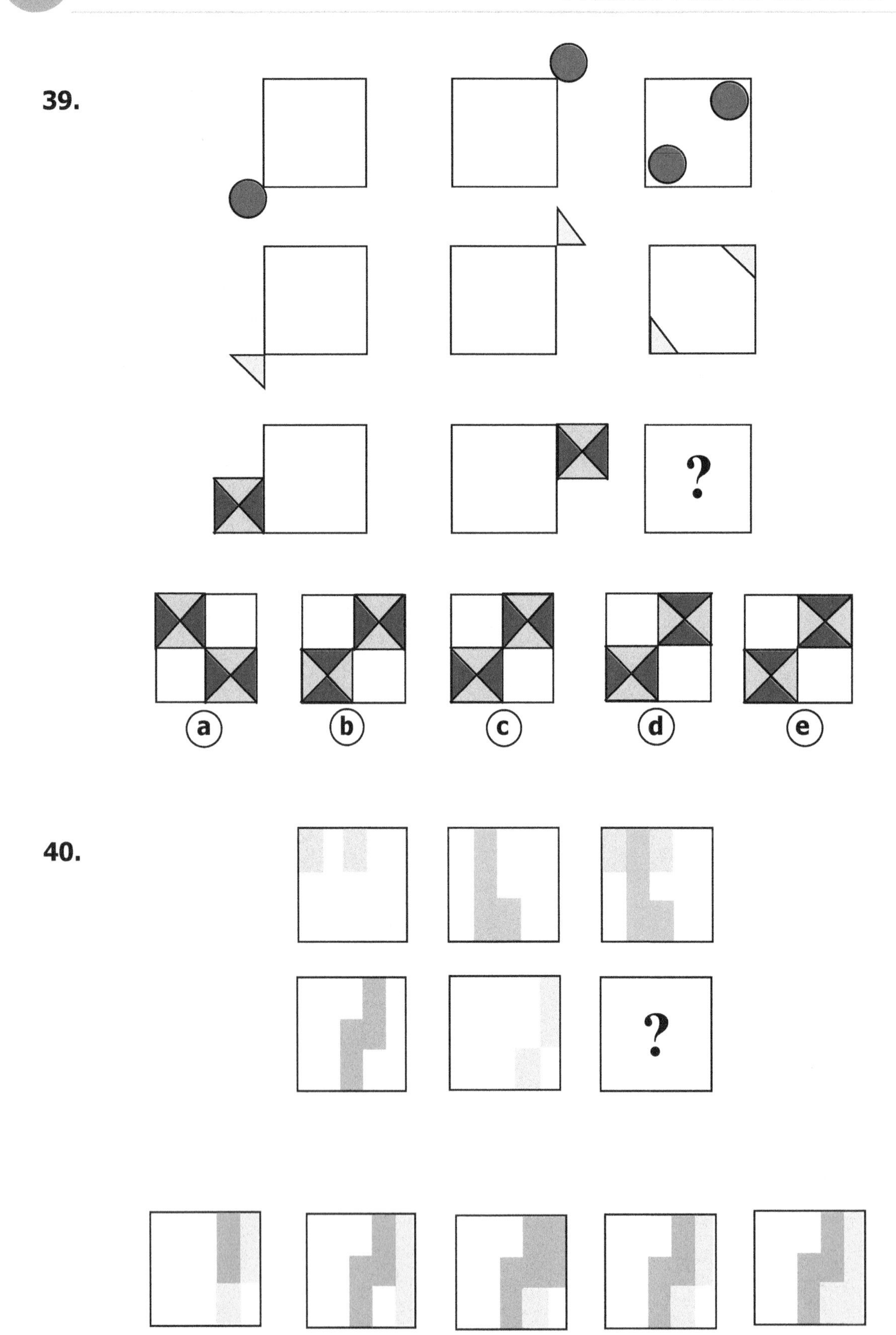

41.

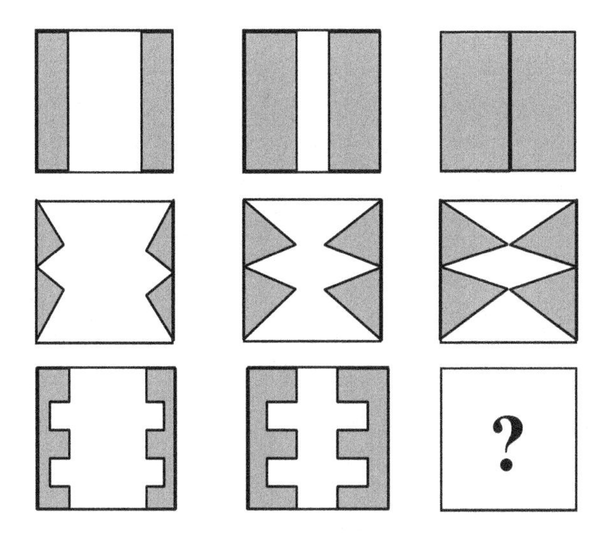

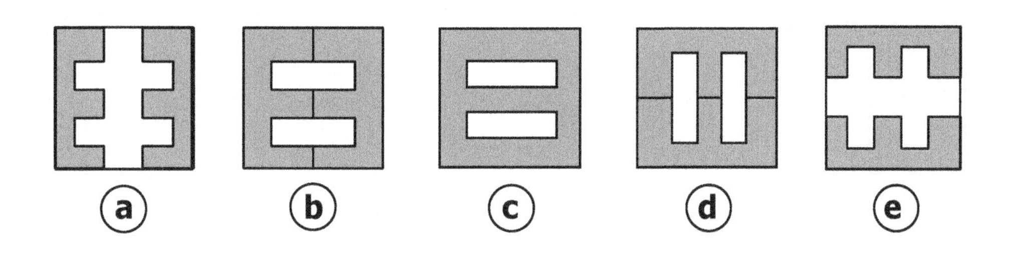

42.

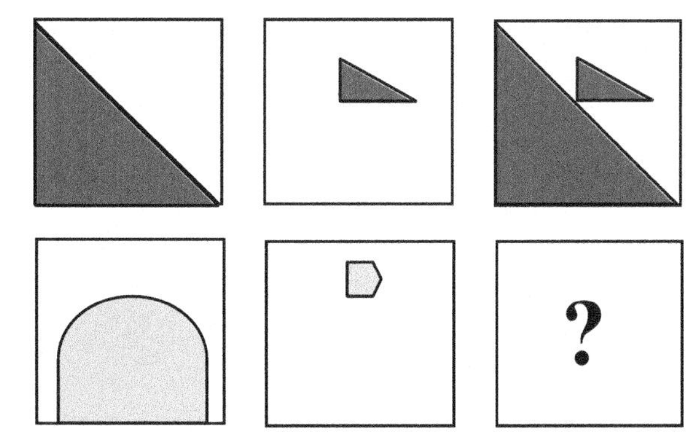

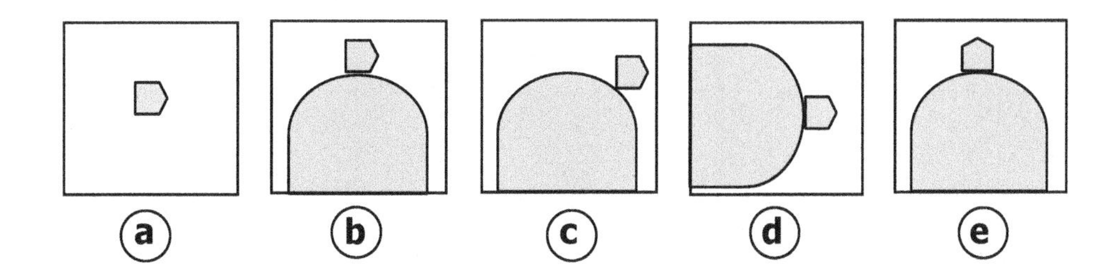

43.

44.

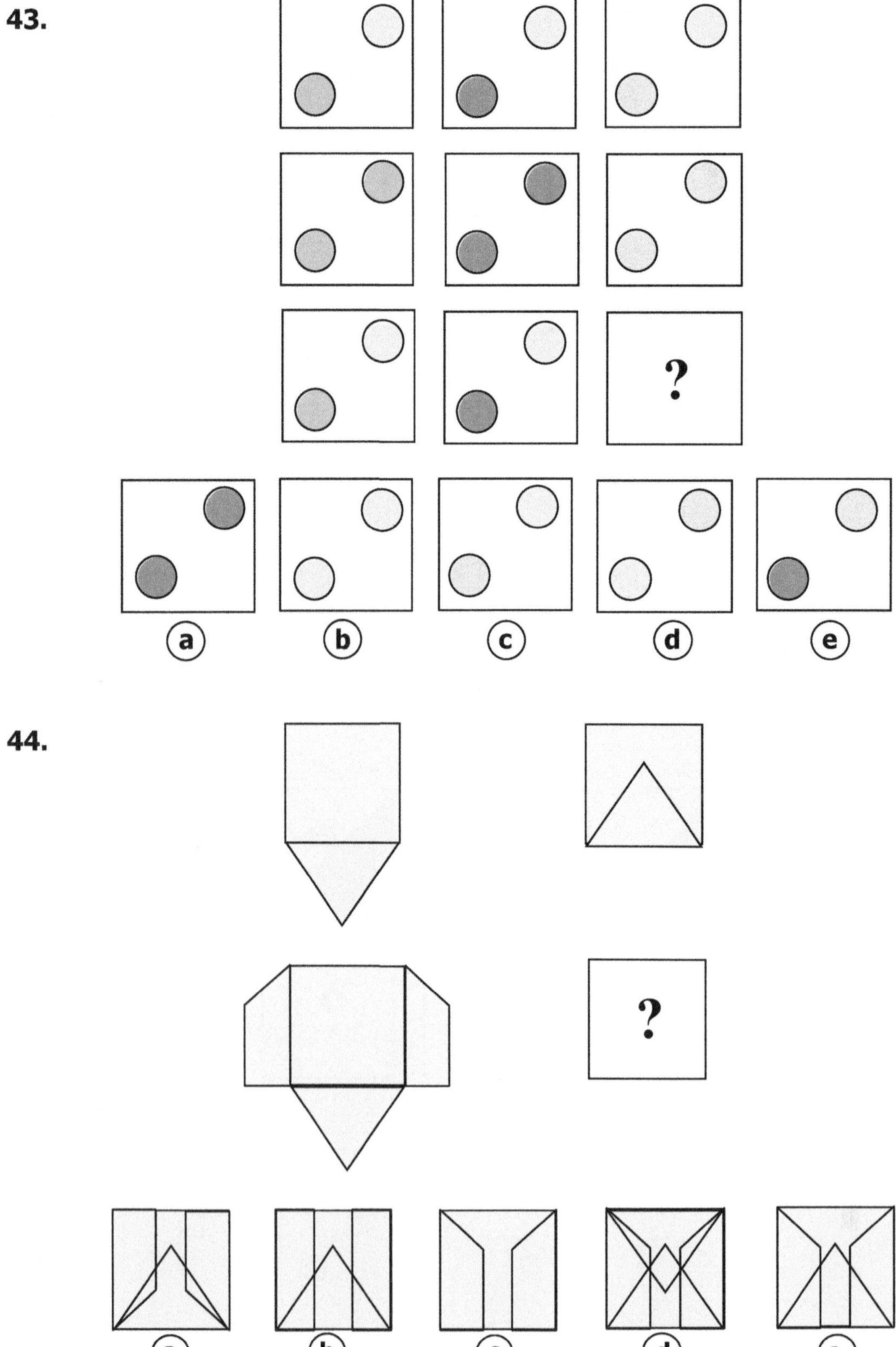

45.

?

a b c d e

46.

?

a b c d e

47.

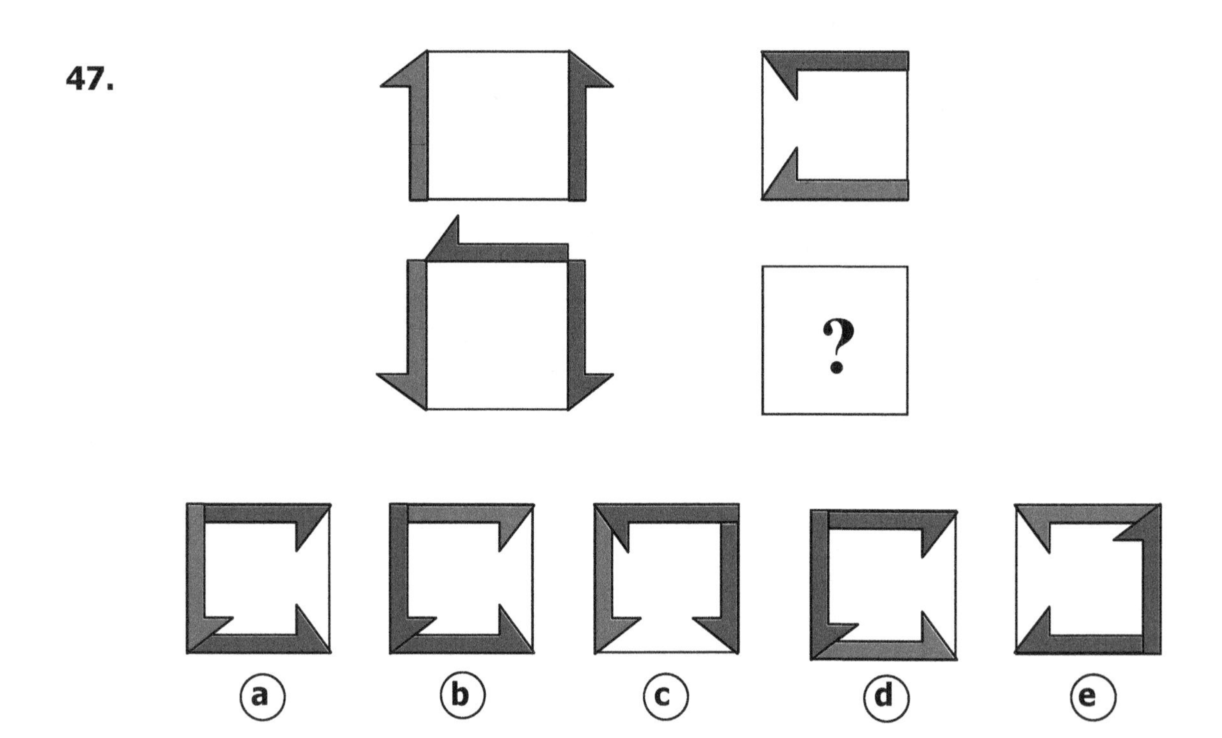

48.

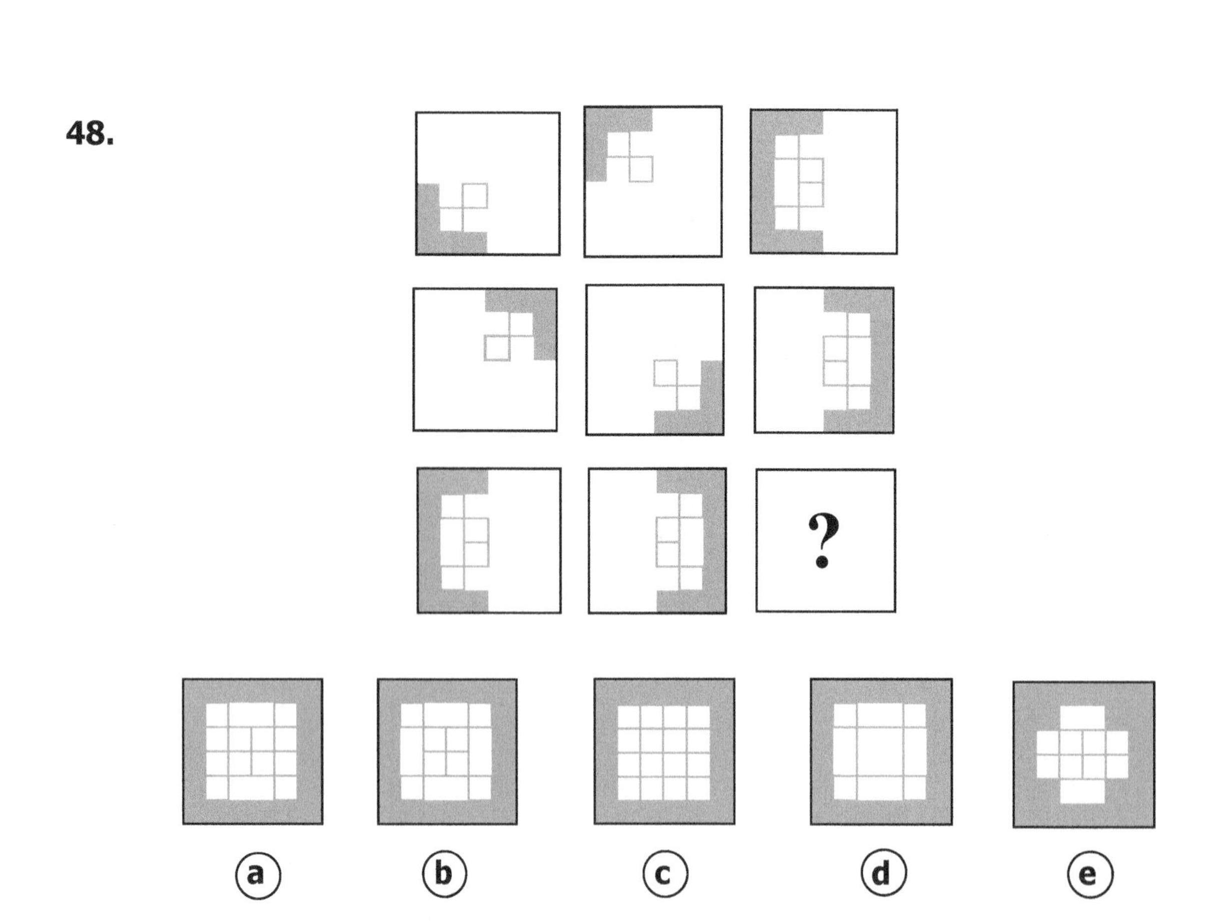

Practice Test

Bonus Questions

1.

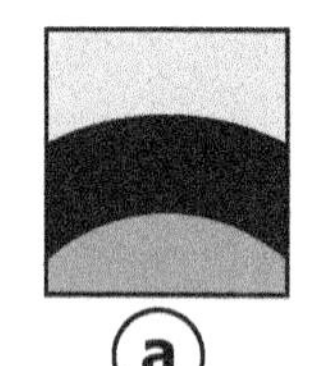
(a)

(b)

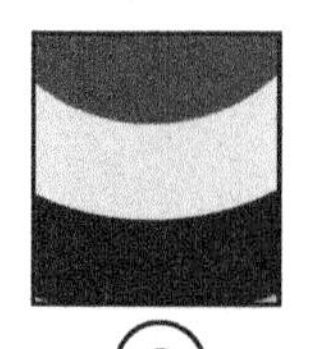
(c)

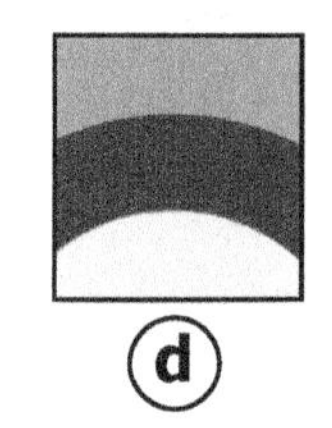
(d)

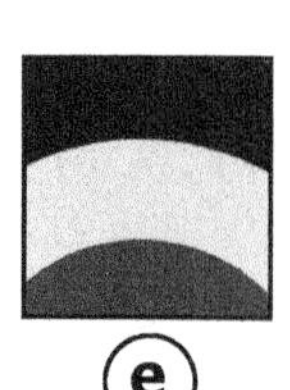
(e)

2.

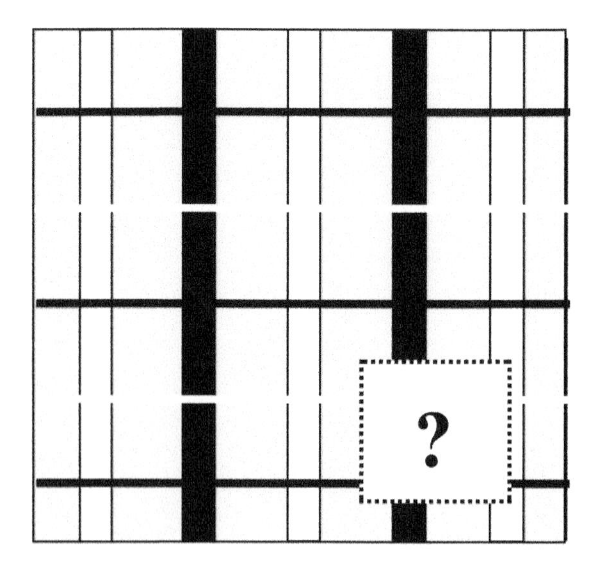

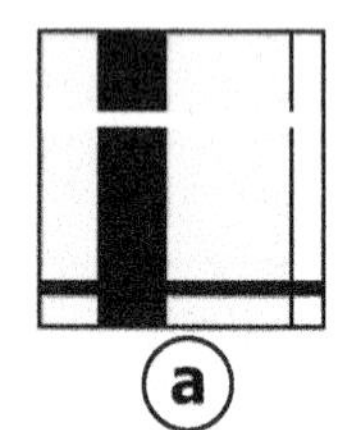
(a)

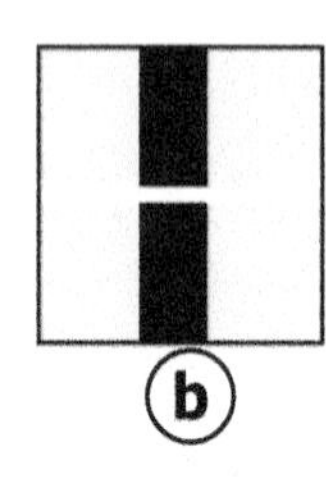
(b)

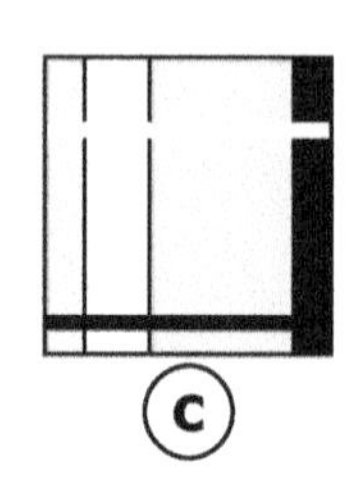
(c)

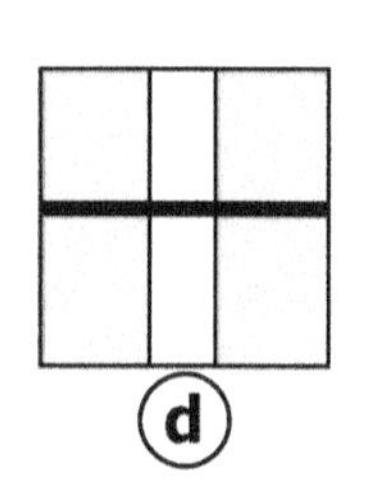
(d)

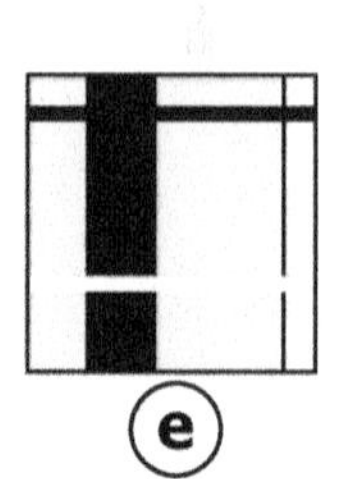
(e)

3.

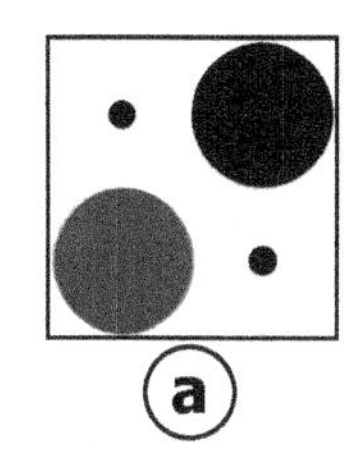

(a)

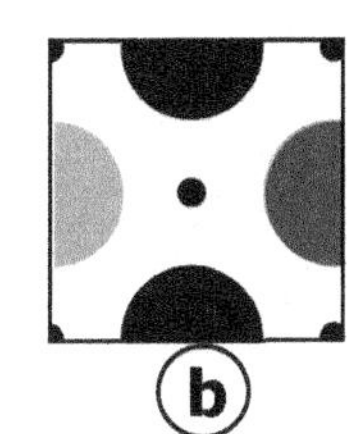

(b)

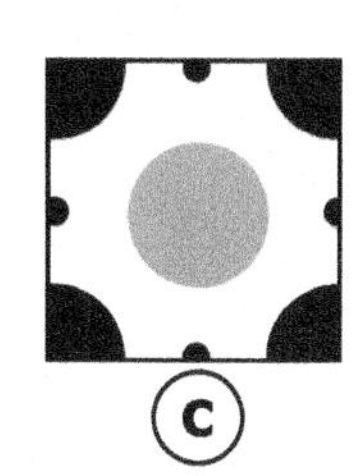

(c)

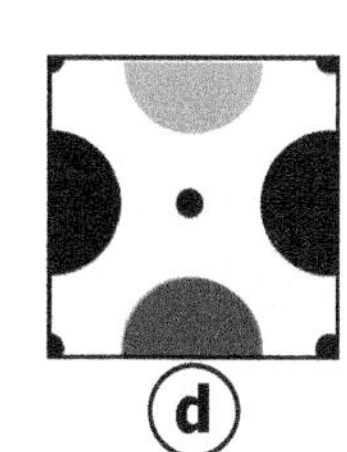

(d)

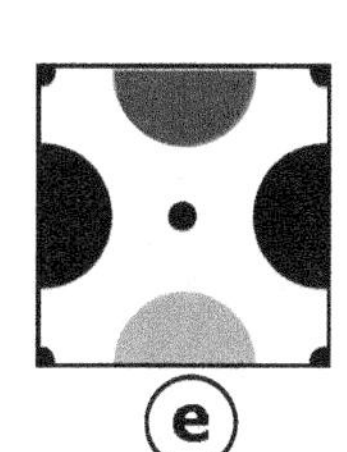

(e)

4.

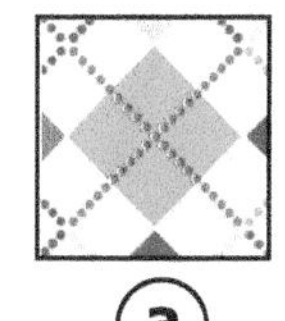

(a)

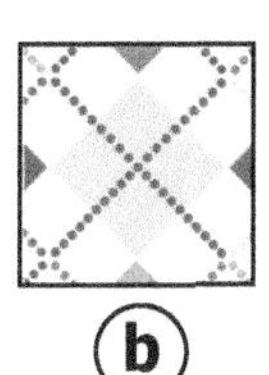

(b)

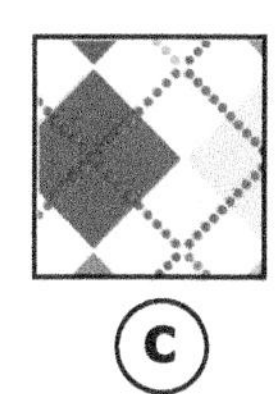

(c)

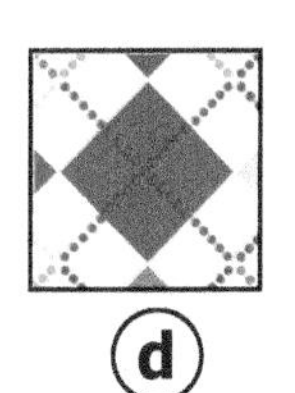

(d)

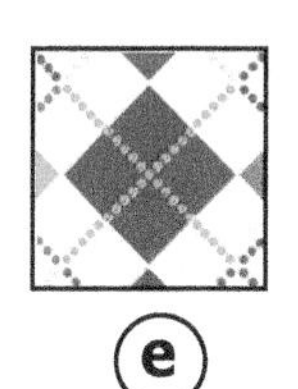

(e)

5.

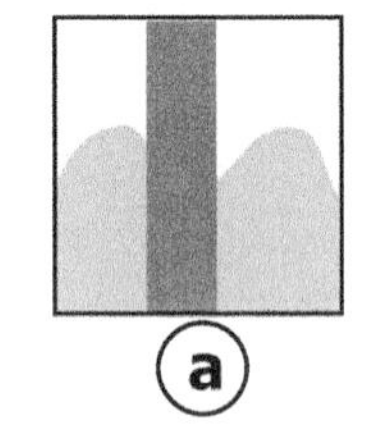
a

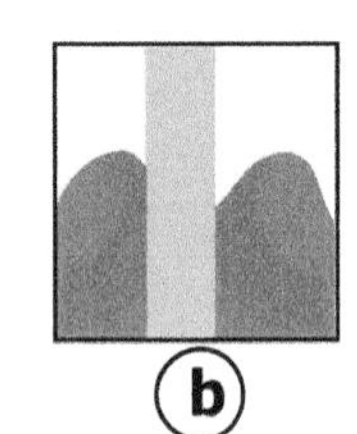
b

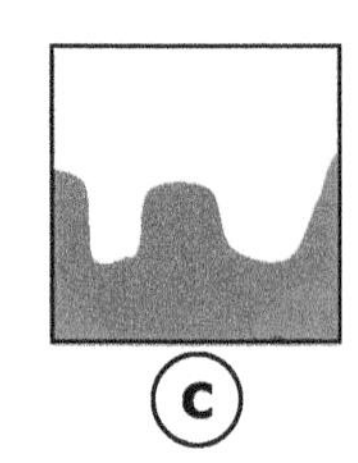
c

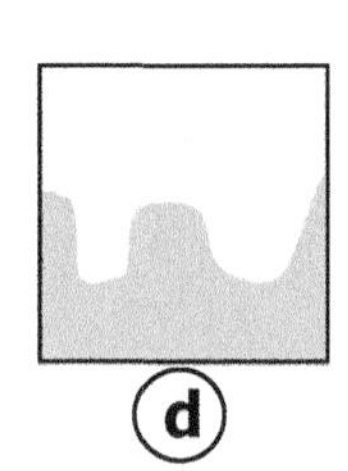
d

e

6.

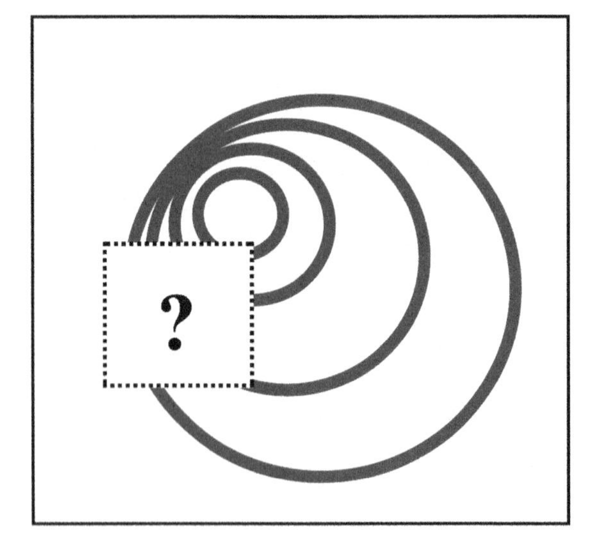

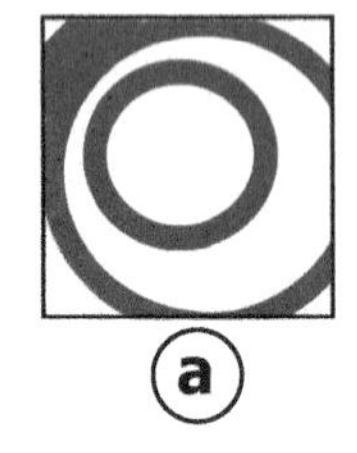
a

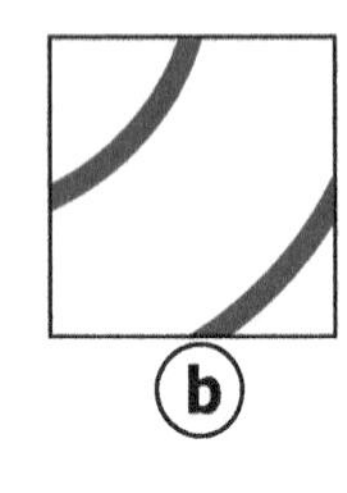
b

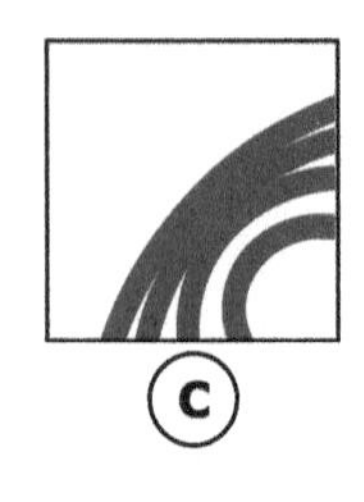
c

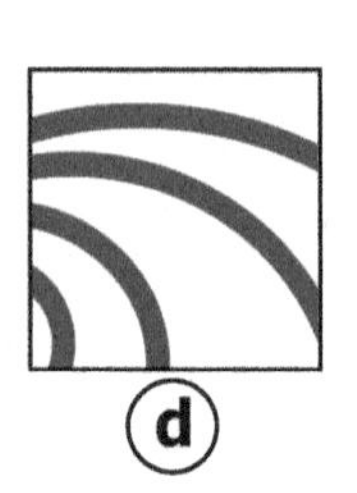
d

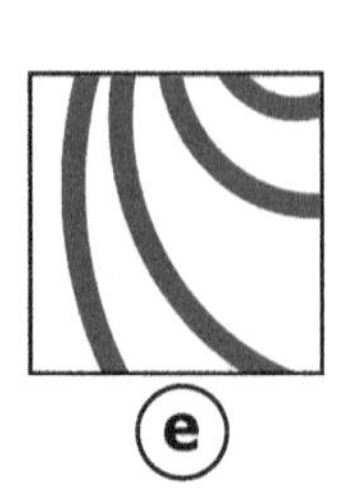
e

7.

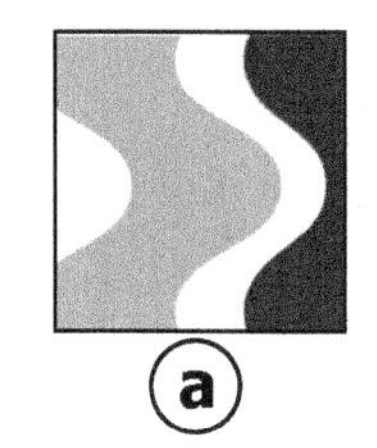
(a)

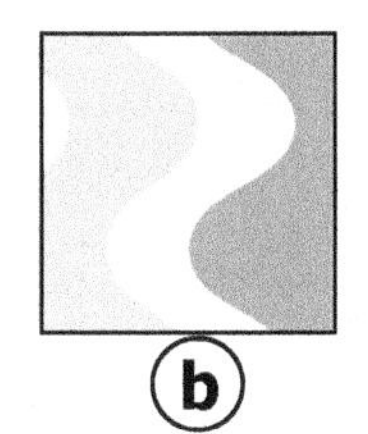
(b)

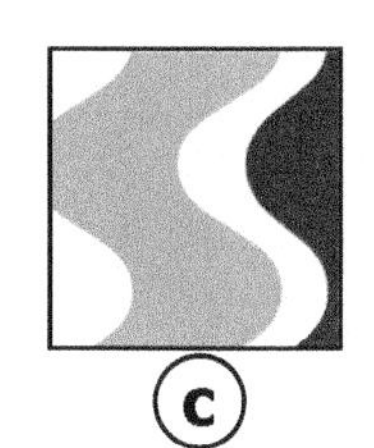
(c)

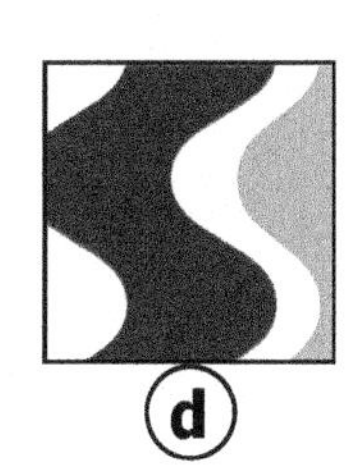
(d)

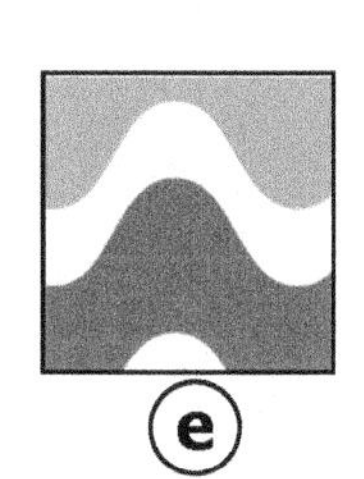
(e)

8.

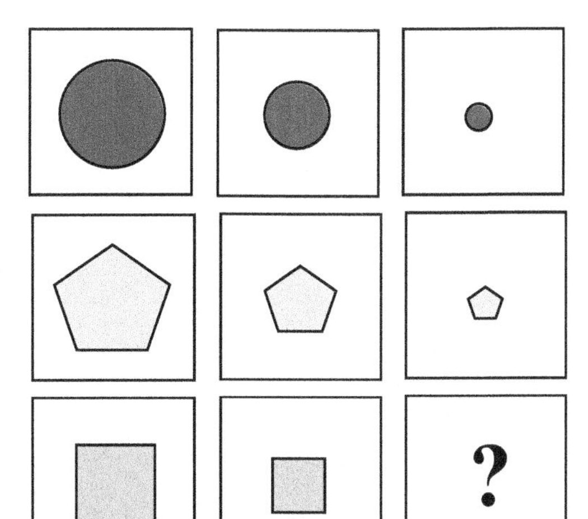

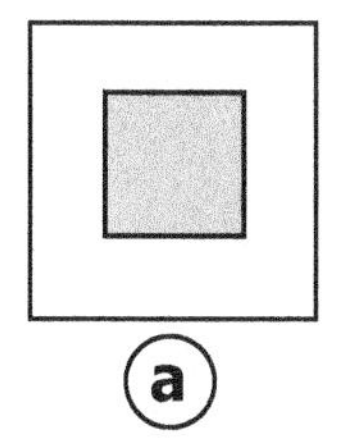
(a)

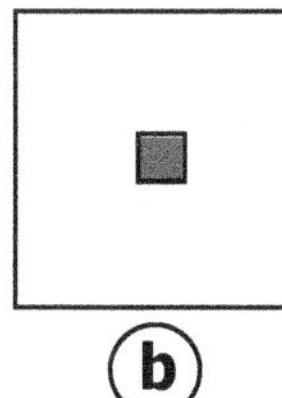
(b)

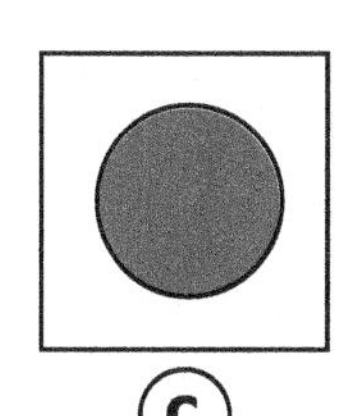
(c)

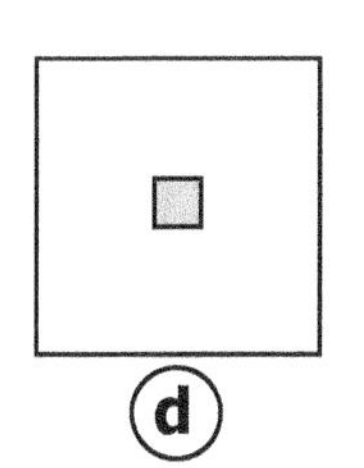
(d)

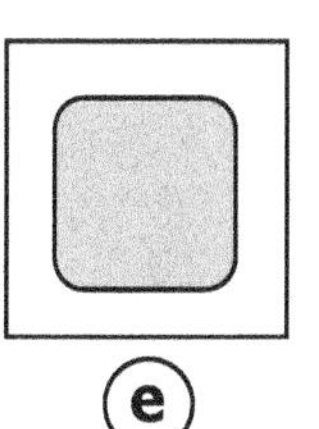
(e)

9.

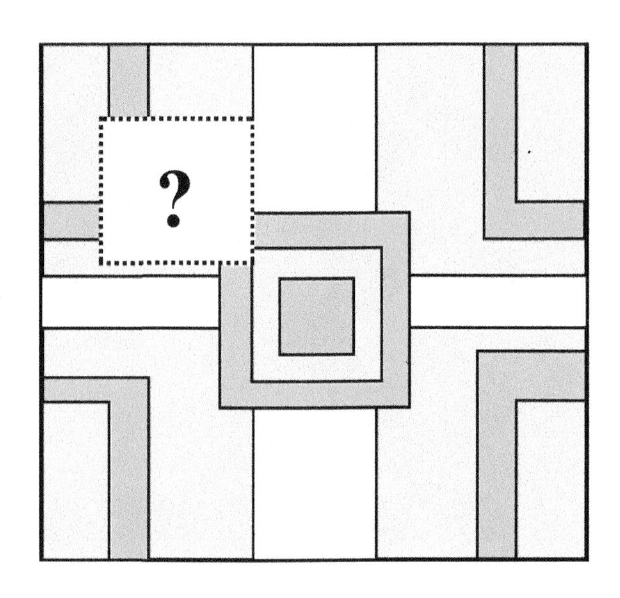

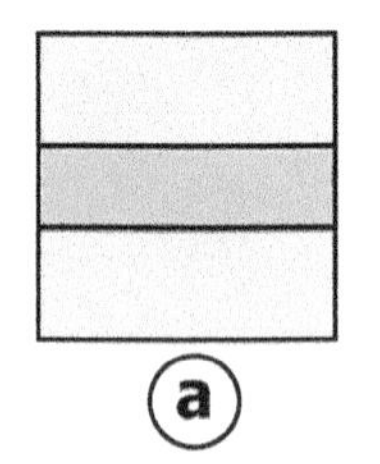
(a)

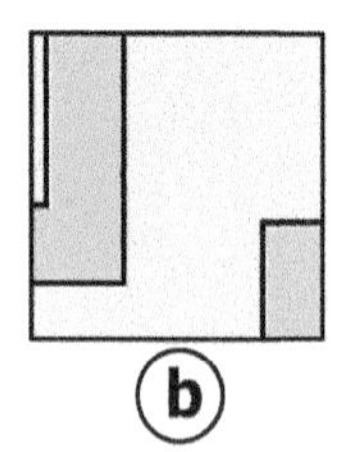
(b)

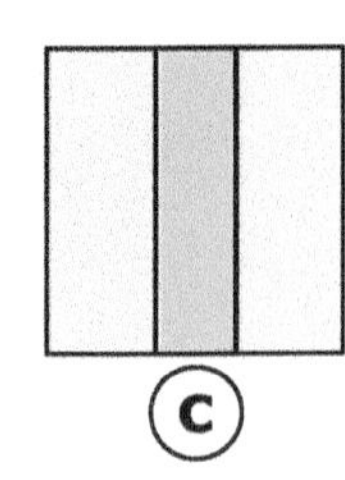
(c)

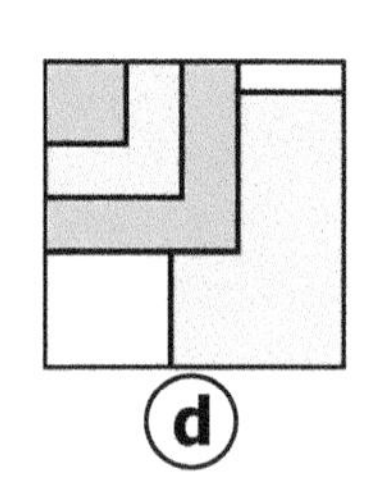
(d)

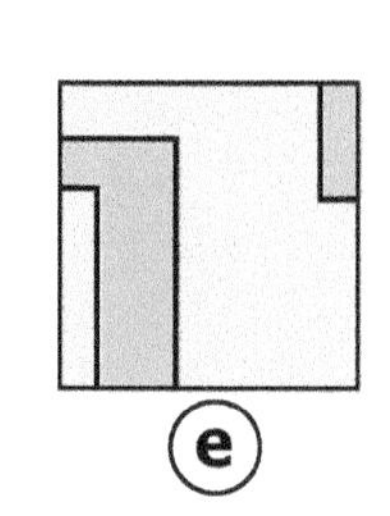
(e)

10.

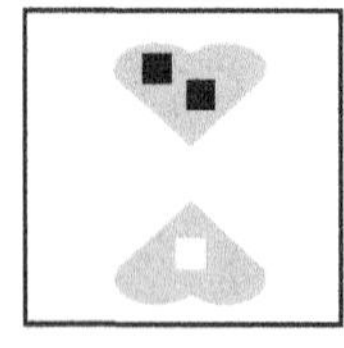

?

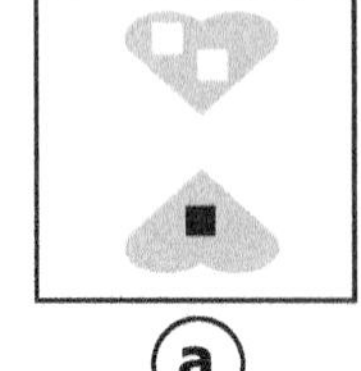
(a)

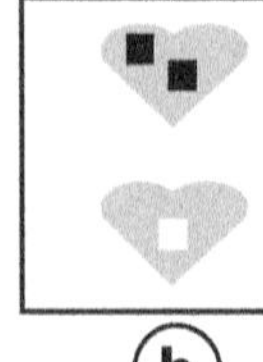
(b)

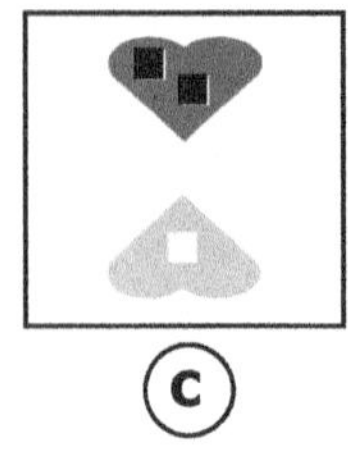
(c)

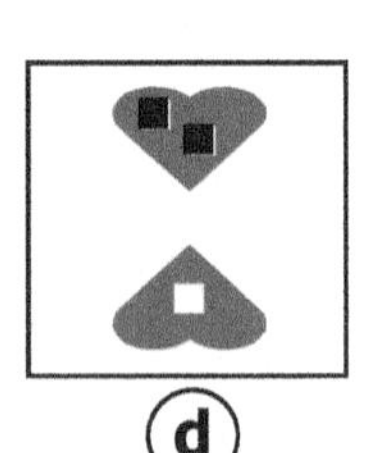
(d)

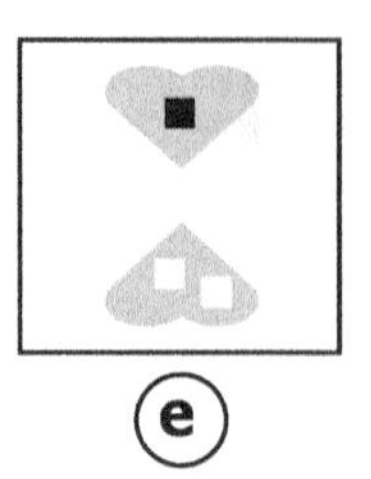
(e)

11.

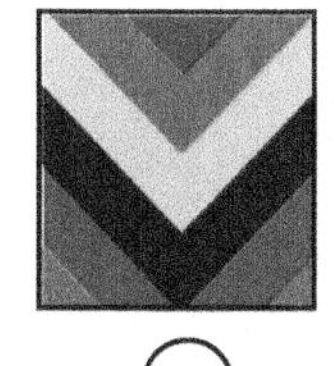

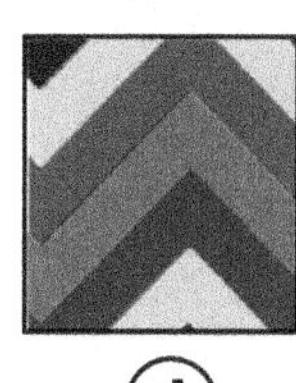

(a) (b) (c) (d) (e)

12.

?

(a) (b) (c) (d) (e)

13.

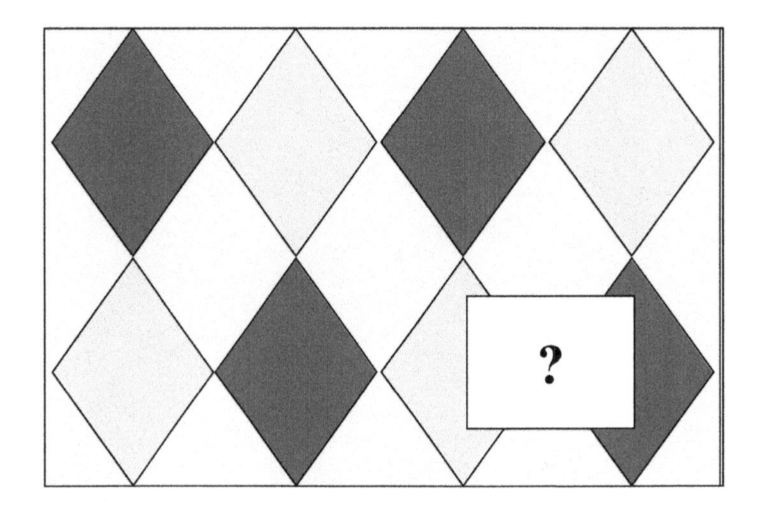

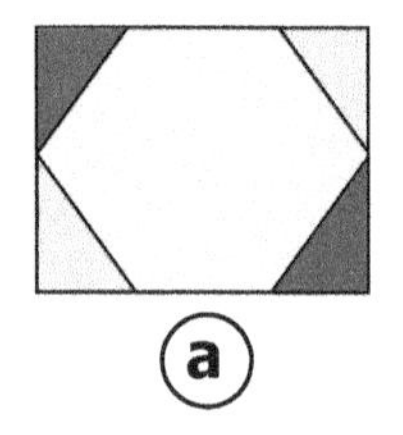
a

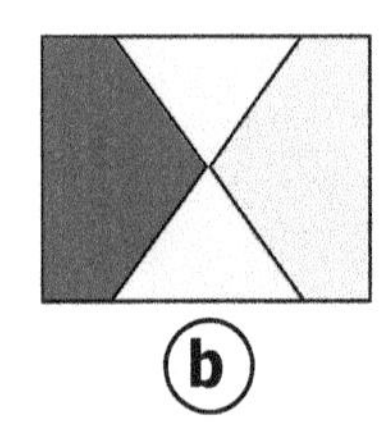
b

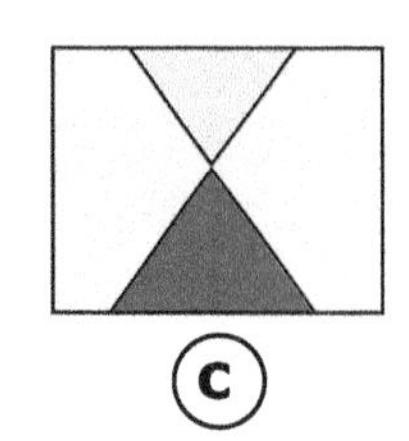
c

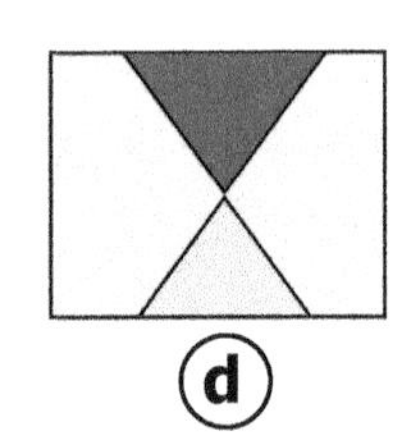
d

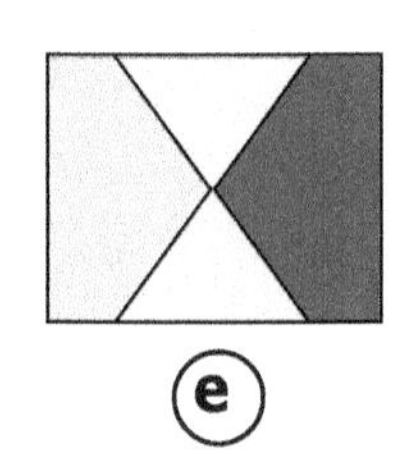
e

14.

a

b

c

d

e

15.

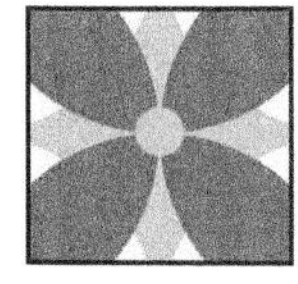

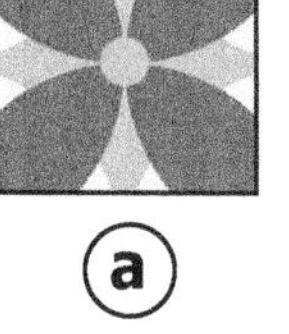

ⓐ

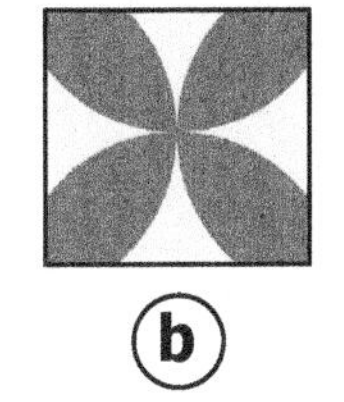

ⓑ

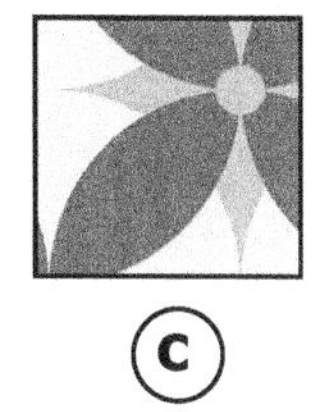

ⓒ

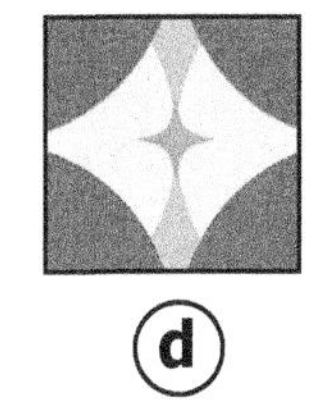

ⓓ

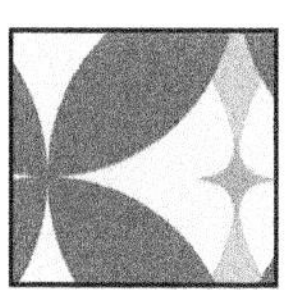

ⓔ

16.

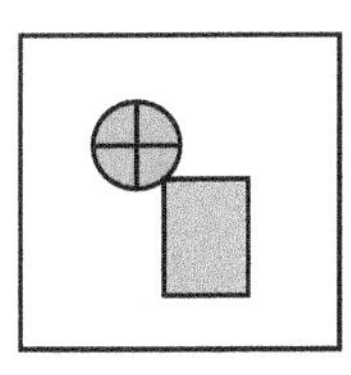

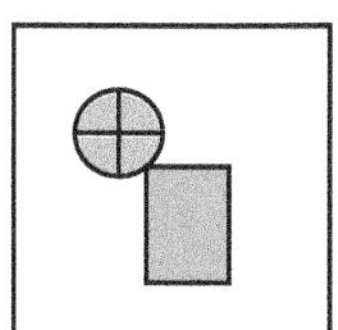

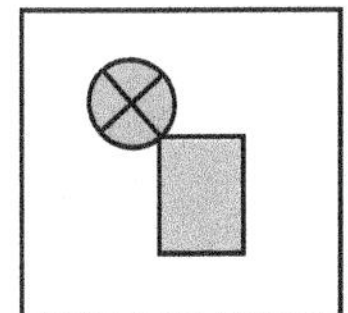

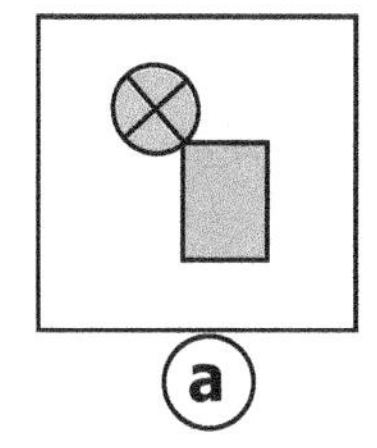

ⓐ

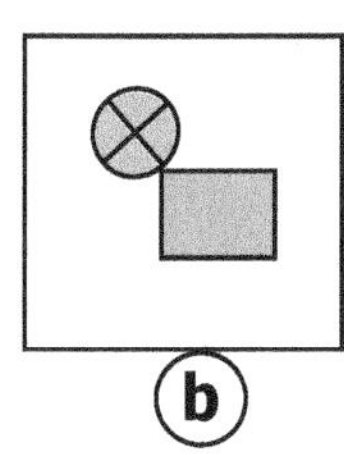

ⓑ

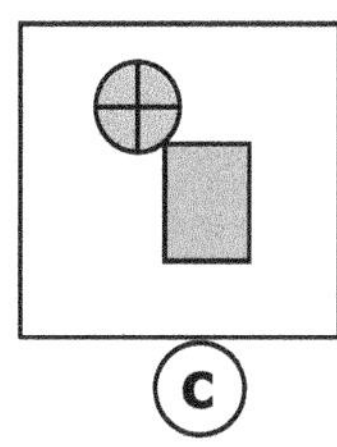

ⓒ

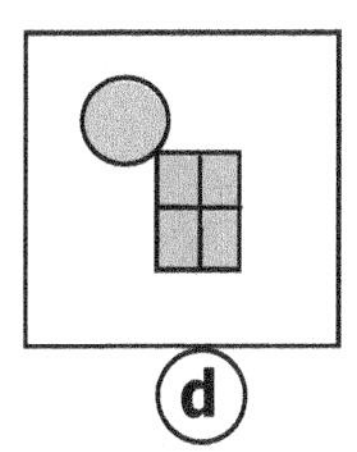

ⓓ

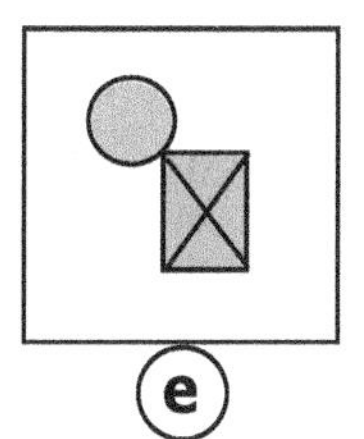

ⓔ

1. b
2. d
3. d
4. d
5. b
6. b
7. a
8. a
9. b
10. e
11. b
12. d
13. a
14. d
15. e
16. b
17. c
18. e
19. d
20. e
21. a
22. c
23. b
24. b
25. a
26. b
27. b
28. e
29. a
30. b
31. c
32. c
33. c
34. c
35. c
36. b
37. e
38. d
39. c
40. d
41. b
42. b
43. c
44. e
45. b
46. c
47. d
48. b

1. e
2. a
3. e
4. d
5. d
6. e
7. c
8. d
9. b
10. a
11. c
12. d
13. e
14. c
15. b
16. a

CPSIA information can be obtained
at www.ICGtesting.com
Printed in the USA
LVOW05s1012230118
563682LV00021B/372/P

9 780982 870884